GROWING FOR FREEZING

Marshall Cavendish London & New York

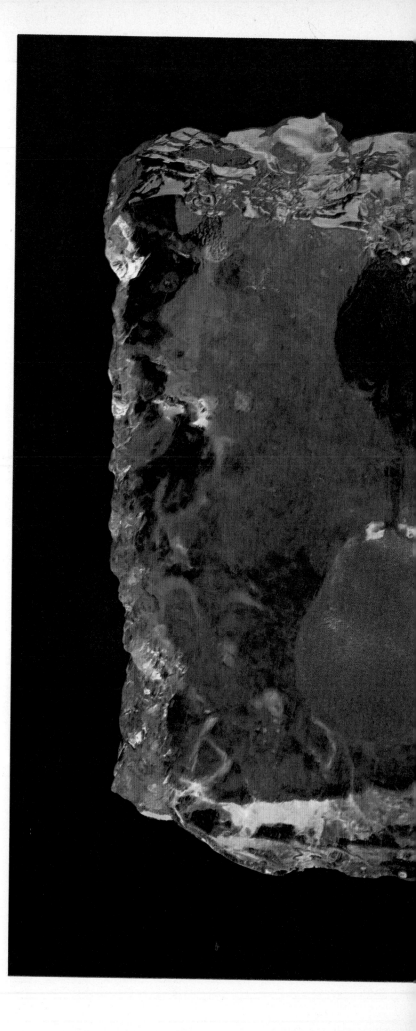

Pictures supplied by:
A-Z Botanical Collection: 24(l), 31(b), 58(c)
B. Alfieri: 35(tl), 82(b)
Amateur Gardening: 65(cr)
D. Arminson: 44(b)
Barnabys: 20(l), 36(b), 64(b)
Steve Bicknall: 51
R. J. Corbin: 19(br), 21, 28, 32, 38(l), 39(r), 40, 41,
    49(b), 52(l), 79(c), 85(t), 85(c)
J. Downward: 57
A. Denney: 54(b), 59(l)
Alan Duns: 8, 9, 24(r), 30(t), 36(t), 37, 49(t), 52(r),
    60, 61(b)
B. Estall: 42(b)
V. Finnis: 33(r), 56(t), 62, 81(t)
B. Furner: 18, 19(tr), 30(b), 34, 48, 78
P. Genereux: 65(tl)
P. Hunt: 55(b)
G. Hyde: 11(c), 29(r), 56(b), 58(b), 73(tr), 76(l), 82(t)
L. Johns: 23(r)
Paul Kemp: 4/5, 47, 77(b)
Don Last: 15, 71(l)
Mansell: 53(t), 53(b), 71(r)
David Meldrum: 14(l), 16, 17, 64(t)
H. Morrison: 56(l)
Roger Phillips: Front Cover, End Papers, 2/3, 6, 7(b),
    10, 11(t), 11(b), 13, 19(bl), 25(r), 35(b), 39(l), 43, 59(r),
    61(t), 66(r), 67, 76(r), 79(t), 81(b), 83, 86/7
Picturepoint: 22, 68, 74(r)
R. Procter: 35(tr), 85(b)
Iain Reed: 26, 38(r), 45
E. Satchell: 58(t)
David Smith: 7(t), 42(t)
D. Smith: 69, 70(b), 73(l), 73(br), 74(l), 75, 79(b), 80(b)
H. Smith: 14(r), 20(r), 23(l), 25(l), 27, 31(t), 33(l), 44(t),
    46, 65(tr), 65(br), 70(t), 77(t), 80(t), 84
Tourist Photo Library: 55(t)
Transworld: 12
The packaging materials on page 8 were supplied
by Frigicold Ltd., 166 Dukes Road, Western Avenue,
London W3 0TJ

Designer Caroline Austin
Author/Editor Renny Harrop

Published by Marshall Cavendish Books Limited,
58 Old Compton Street, London W1V 5PA

ISBN 0 85685 172 8

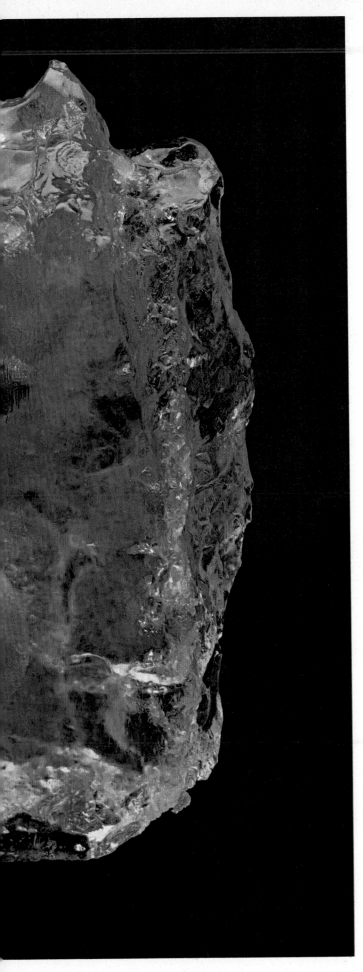

Introduction

Growing for Freezing is for people who care about what they eat.

Home-grown vegetables and fruit are generally of better quality than those available in the shops —mainly because they are much fresher and can be picked in their prime. Whether your garden is small or large, there is almost sure to be sufficient space to grow most of the crops included in this book. Fruit trees can be grown against walls, herbs in pots and window boxes, and vegetables, such as artichokes, lettuces and runner beans, look very attractive interspersed among flowers.

The best method of preserving your carefully cultivated produce is by freezing, because, in terms of flavour, texture and colour, frozen food bears the closest resemblance to fresh food. Freezing means that you will have a supply of food, in top condition, available throughout the year.

This book explains, with clear step-by-step instructions, exactly how to care for your vegetables, fruits and herbs. It includes everything—from planting the seed, through cultivation and harvesting, to preparation and freezing.

The selection of food crops included is very wide. All of them have been chosen for their ease of cultivation and suitability to freezing. The end result is a book that will enable you to use your garden AND your freezer to produce and preserve food of high quality with the minimum effort and maximum efficiency.

Contents

Breaking
the ice

The superiority of home-grown produce over commercially-grown crops is undeniable. That freezing is the best way of preserving food is equally true. Put the two together and you have a combination that will provide you with a varied selection of prime fruit and vegetables throughout the year, regardless of season.

With food prices soaring daily, growing for freezing makes economic sense too. The cost involved in buying a few pieces of basic gardening equipment is minimal. The cost of a freezer is of course much higher, but this will be quickly repaid if you learn to use it to its best advantage.

As well as being cheaper, home-grown produce tastes better than commercially-grown produce, which is selected for its high yield, its resistance to pests and diseases and the ease of production rather than for culinary merit or taste. The valuable time lost between harvesting and bringing the food to your table also inevitably affects the quality.

When you don't have to worry about such criteria you can concentrate on growing food for flavour alone. For the home gardener this presents few problems and is no more difficult to grow, but the difference in taste is enormous. You can choose to grow particular varieties which are simply not economic to the commercial producer and also fruit and vegetables which are becoming increasingly difficult to buy on the open market.

Even so, without a freezer, some waste is inevitable. Vegetables or fruit which mature all at the same time either have to be given away to friends and neighbours or left to rot where they are. Now you can pick each crop as and when it is ready and freeze what you don't need. This will give you the luxury of being able to eat out of season crops without paying the prohibitive prices normally involved.

Gone are the long trips to the greengrocers, returning laden with heavy baskets. Now you have only to walk outside to your garden or open up your freezer and select whatever food you require. Fresh vegetables and fruit inevitably involve some time in their preparation; this is no longer necessary when they are frozen. All the groundwork has already been done and you have only to decide whether to cook them briefly first or eat them as they are. By following the section on the growing and freezing of herbs as well, you will be able to produce a meal in minutes with that touch of distinction, flavour and presentation normally only associated with a first-class restaurant. Incidentally, any technical terms used in the instructions are fully explained in the glossary at the back.

The amount of time you need to spend in the garden is very little, perhaps an hour or two a week, while the time you save shopping and in the kitchen is halved. In fact, growing food for your freezer means that you have increased hours of leisure available and the extra money to enjoy them, knowing that you are well stocked with food preserved in the most hygenic way with all its goodness and flavour intact.

Top *Pumpkins are best frozen after they have been cooked and puréed. After thawing, the purée is ready for use either as a side vegetable or as an instant filling for pumpkin pie.*

Above *Tomatoes, onions, parsley and tarragon are all suitable for freezing. Tomatoes, however, cannot be used as a salad vegetable after freezing but are perfectly good for grilling, frying and in soups and stews.*

Left *A selection of fruit, vegetables and herbs which can all be grown with relative ease. Picked fresh from the garden, they reach the table in perfect condition. Frozen like this, they will provide delicious, economical meals throughout the year regardless of season.*

7

Freezing

Freezing is the simplest, most efficient and natural way of preserving food. The flavour, appearance and texture remain the same and the nutritional value of the food is virtually unchanged.

As owners of freezers you will already be aware of the many advantages that this form of storage provides, and also of the simple rules which need to be followed in order to run your freezer economically and at maximum efficiency.

However, the two points which need to be taken seriously into account when freezing your own produce deserve full explanation. They are the principle of 'fast freezing' and the importance of correct wrapping.

Fast freezing

The sooner a product is frozen, the better its qualities will be preserved. This is because all food contains water which when frozen forms ice-crystals which expand and destroy the cell structure. The faster food is frozen the smaller the crystals.

Below *A selection of the equipment necessary for the successful freezing of your home-grown produce. A freezer knife, thermometer and ice-cube tray are illustrated as well as a wide range of commercially available wrapping materials. The wire mesh basket in the centre is for blanching.*

Most freezers have a control which may be labelled fast freeze, auto-freeze or super cold. When switched on, this overrides the thermostat and reduces the normal storage temperature of $-18°C$ ($0°F$) to $-34°C$ ($-30°F$).

Switch this on an hour or two before you start to freeze and leave it on until the food is rock hard.

Wrapping food for freezing

No matter what type of freezer you have, or how perfect the condition of your produce, the wrapping material in which you enclose the food is of enormous importance. If food is packaged incorrectly, the very low temperature of the air in the freezer will eventually dry it out and make it tasteless and unpleasant to eat. Inadequate wrapping also leads to cross-flavouring.

Freezer packaging materials are moisture- and vapour-proof, and resistant to breakage at low temperature. The materials are available from freezer suppliers, large stationers and department stores or direct from the manufacturers. Bear in mind that rectangular containers are easier to stack and take up less room than circular ones. If you wash and treat them carefully you should be able to use most containers again and again. When buying, take the overall volume of the container into consideration. There is no point in acquiring enormous containers if you are freezing food for a family of four. The range of materials is wide and includes the following:

Polythene or plastic bags Use 120–200 gauge bags made for this purpose as these will not tear. They are re-usable, come in a variety of shapes and sizes and can be used for all foods. Placing a bag inside a rigid container before filling and freezing will result in a shape suitable for stacking.

Special 'boiling bags' are available which are similar to plastic bags but are specially heat-treated. They are very useful for fruit and vegetables as they enable you to cook food in its wrapping straight from the freezer.

Plastic boxes Ideal for most food and liquids, plastic boxes are easy to use and stack well. The more rigid the container the better the lid will fit.

Waxed cartons These are rigid, waxed cardboard containers which are ideal for fruit and vegetables, whether in liquid or solid form. Although they are available in a variety of shapes and sizes, it is nevertheless more convenient to use rectangular rather than round containers. Make sure that the lids are well sealed and do not fill with hot liquid as the wax will melt and the box become porous.

Foil This should be heavy duty or freezer aluminium foil, although ordinary household foil is adequate for short-term freezing. The longer the roll, the more economical it will be.

Shaped foil dishes These lightweight, re-usable dishes are available in a variety of shapes and sizes. Those that have their own foil lids can be frozen direct, otherwise seal with foil and enclose in a plastic bag. The fact that they can be used for freezing, cooking and serving their contents, makes them extremely practical.

Interleaving Some fruits and vegetables are easier to thaw if they have been packed with layers of greaseproof paper, foil or plastic in between them to prevent them from sticking to one another.

Clear plastic wrapping This is similar to foil but is transparent. It is available in rolls and generally comes in a box with a serrated cutting edge. Some types are self-adhesive while other varieties will need to be sealed with tape. The advantage of see-through wrapping is that it allows you to identify the contents quickly and means that you can put the label on the inside or the outside. Food wrapped in clear wrap does, however, need a second covering, such as a plastic bag.

Below *Fresh fruit in perfect condition may be frozen intact. Slightly damaged or over-ripe fruit should be made into a purée beforehand.*

Bottom *The majority of vegetables should be blanched before freezing. This process is not necessary for herbs.*

9

Reaping the benefit

The increasing cost of buying both fresh and frozen vegetables has made growing and freezing your own produce an extremely attractive alternative. Most gardens, however small, can accommodate a small vegetable patch and the cost of seeds and equipment is minimal. When you also take into account the vast improvement in the flavour of home-grown vegetables, the sheer convenience of being able to select a vegetable at need by simply walking outside or opening your freezer, and the sense of satisfaction gained from producing your own food, the attractions are enormous.

Even if you already grow your own vegetables, freezing them adds a new dimension to your diet and avoids many of the disadvantages previously experienced. Gluts of peas will no longer produce a cry of 'Oh no, not peas again!' Freeze them, and enjoy their delicious flavour during the winter when the choice of fresh vegetables is strictly limited. Nor will your carefully cultivated produce have time to become coarse and tasteless because it will be frozen while it is in prime condition, clearing space in the process for more and different crops.

The list of vegetables included in this section is not intended to be completely comprehensive. There are certain vegetables which simply do not freeze well and others which involve so much time and care in their cultivation that we have decided to exclude them. Conversely, many of the vegetables included are available throughout the year, while others can be stored for long periods of time. They are listed because freezing is by far the best way of retaining the flavour, texture and nutritive value of a vegetable and it is also far quicker, for instance, to reheat frozen spinach purée than to pick, wash, chop and cook spinach from scratch.

The vegetables have been listed in alphabetical order for easy reference, and for the same reason we have chosen to place the instructions for growing and freezing them under one heading. If a heading has been omitted, this is because it is not applicable to that particular vegetable. No specific dates have been given because weather conditions are so variable and because being able to freeze your own produce makes the timing of successional crops less important.

The main thing to remember is that no matter how superb a vegetable may be, the method of freezing it is of paramount importance and the instructions should be followed very carefully. Also a vegetable that is only second-rate when fresh will be third-rate after freezing. Always harvest when the vegetable is young and tender and only in amounts small enough for you to be able to prepare and freeze it as soon as possible after picking.

Blanching

You will notice that under the freezing instructions a blanching time is given in most cases. This needs some explanation. Blanching means scalding in boiling water for a specific amount of time. The object of

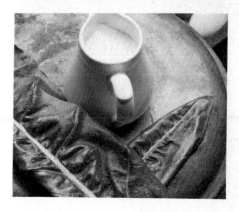

Above and left *Vegetables should always be picked when they are young and tender and not left to grow coarse and woody, particularly if you are going to freeze them. As their flavour quickly deteriorates after harvesting, pick vegetables in small quantities at a time and prepare for cooking or freezing with as little delay as possible.*

Above *Because home-grown vegetables are harvested by hand rather than machine, you can choose to grow varieties for their flavour rather than for convenience.*

Right *Freezing vegetables uncooked allows you to decide how you wish to use them as and when the need arises. It is, however, perfectly possible to freeze cooked vegetable dishes, such as the soup in this picture, and know that you have something in store which needs no other preparation than thawing, reheating and seasoning.*

this is to retard the action of the enzymes, present in all vegetables, which would otherwise cause deterioration in colour, flavour and texture, even at sub zero temperatures. The time depends on the size and type of vegetable and where applicable, this is listed under the appropriate heading. Take great care – over-blanching and under-blanching are both equally harmful.

Here is a list of the equipment you will need:

A pan large enough to hold about $4\frac{1}{2}$ litres (8 pints) of water, e.g. a preserving pan

An immersing container for holding the vegetables in water, e.g. the wire basket from a chip pan or a nylon wine-straining bag

A kitchen clock for timing the blanching process

A bowl of ice-cold water

A sieve or colander for draining the vegetables after chilling

The method is simple and always the same:

1   Prepare and weigh the vegetables and separate into divisions of $\frac{1}{2}$kg(1lb).

2   Bring the water to the boil, allowing $4\frac{1}{2}$ litres (8 pints) of water to each $\frac{1}{2}$kg(1lb) of vegetables.

3   Place the vegetables in the basket or bag and immerse in the water.

4   Return the water to the boil within one minute and then time according to the instructions.

5   Remove and plunge the vegetables into a previously prepared bowl of chilled water.

6   Drain and cool to room temperature. Pack and place in the freezer immediately.

The same blanching water may be used for about six to eight batches, this saves fuel and helps to prevent loss of nutrients.

Vegetables that have been blanched before freezing cook in approximately one-third to one-half the time needed when fresh. Ideally vegetables treated in this way should be cooked straight from the freezer in a small quantity of boiling water or hot melted butter.

It is worth noting that most major seed producers recommend specific varieties of each vegetable which are particularly suitable for freezing.

Finally, do not be deterred by what may appear to be a somewhat complex process, once you have frozen your first batch of vegetables, you will realise how easy it really is.

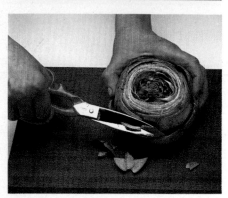

Artichokes, Globe

These plants produce ornamental, thistle-like flower heads, and are often grown for their decorative rather than their culinary use.

How to grow

Soil Rich and well-drained. Dig it over and manure well the autumn previous to planting.

Aspect Sunny and sheltered.

Sowing Sow in an unheated greenhouse in early spring or outdoors in late spring. Thin to 15cm(6in) apart and transplant to their final quarters the following autumn.

Planting Artichokes are much easier to grow from bought offsets. Plant in spring, leaving a space of at least 1m(1yd) between plants in both directions. Protection is necessary in winter in areas susceptible to frost.

Cultivation Tie the leaves up in a clump during the autumn and surround with bracken, straw or other protective material in cold areas. Artichokes need careful watering during dry weather. A bed that is over three years old should be discarded and a new one established. New plants can be produced by cutting suckers from the parent plants in the spring.

Pests and diseases None to worry about.

Harvesting The large flower heads should be gathered just as the sepals begin to open and before any mauve tufts appear. The centre buds are ready first while the side buds tend to mature after the centre bud is cut.

How to freeze

Preparation Remove coarse outer leaves, trim stems and wash thoroughly.

Blanching 7 minutes. A little lemon juice added to the blanching water helps to prevent discoloration.

Packing Pack in rigid containers.

Freezer life 12 months.

To use Cook direct from the freezer in boiling water.

14

Artichokes, Jerusalem

This vegetable is no relation to the globe artichoke nor does it have any connection with the Holy Land. It is an edible tuber related to the sunflower.

How to grow
Soil Most soils that have been well-dug and manured.
Aspect Open and sunny but can be grown in odd corners.
Planting Buy tubers and expose them to light in a protected spot until small green shoots appear. Plant in early spring about 10cm(4in) deep and 45cm(18in) apart in rows 1m(1yd) apart.
Cultivation Although they can remain in the same ground for several years, it is better to replant them every year as this prevents the entanglement of spreading roots. Jerusalem artichokes can be propagated by selecting small tubers from those lifted in early winter and replanting them as soon as possible.
Pests and diseases None to worry about.
Harvesting Begin to lift tubers as soon as they are large enough to eat. They should be used as soon as possible to prevent discoloration.

How to freeze
Preparation Should be frozen in purée form. Scrub, peel and slice. Using a heavy-based saucepan, melt butter over gentle heat in the proportion of 30g(1oz) butter to each $\frac{1}{2}$kg(1lb) of artichokes. Add the artichokes to the pan and cook until they have softened slightly. Add $\frac{1}{2}$ litre (1 pint) of chicken stock and simmer until the vegetables are completely soft. Rub the artichokes through a sieve or liquidize in an electric blender to form a purée.
Packing Pack in rigid containers leaving a headspace.
Freezer life 3 months.
To use Reheat purée straight from freezer in a saucepan over gentle heat. Add milk or cream and seasoning.

Far left *Globe artichokes should be prepared for freezing by trimming the stems and coarse outer leaves, removing the central choke and rubbing cut edges with lemon.*

Top left *Many people grow globe artichokes for their decorative appearance as much as for their culinary value.*

Below left *Serve cooked artichokes with hot, melted butter, vinaigrette or Hollandaise sauce for a perfect first course. Fresh artichokes do not have to be trimmed before cooking.*

Asparagus

This delicious vegetable is expensive to buy but easy to grow. Once established, an asparagus plant will produce stems in the same bed for 20 years.

How to grow

Soil Any rich, well-drained soil. Dig the bed over and fork in compost or manure in the autumn prior to planting.

Aspect Sunny.

Sowing Sow outside in spring 23cm(9in) apart. Thin to 30cm(12in) apart when they reach a height of 10cm(4in). Water during dry weather, and, when the ferny leaves turn yellow, cut them down to ground level. Transplant the following spring to a bed which has been previously prepared, leaving 38cm(15in) between each plant. Make sure that the crowns are about 10cm(4in) below the surface. Do

Below *Whether fresh from the garden or out of the freezer, asparagus needs only the addition of melted butter to make a beautiful vegetable dish.*

Bottom left and right *Before cooking, asparagus stems should first be trimmed and scraped and then divided into bunches according to thickness.*

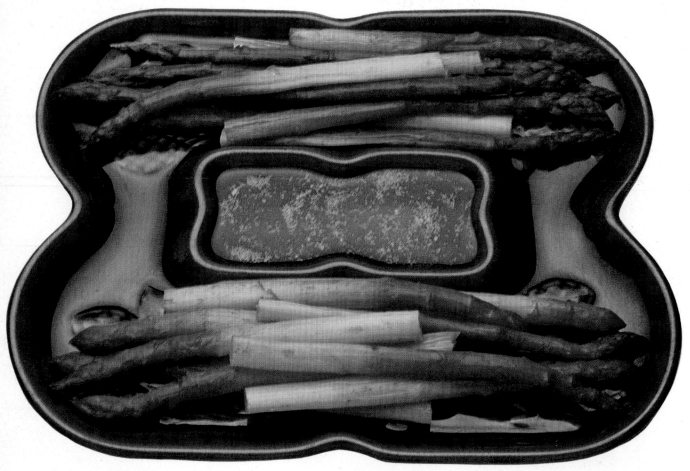

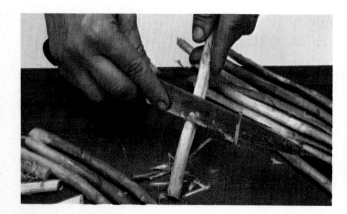

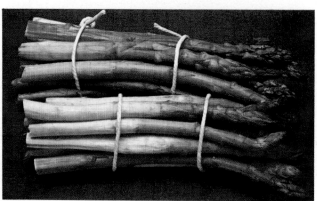

not harvest until the third year after sowing.

Planting It is far simpler and less time-consuming to buy 2-year-old plants in spring from a nursery and transplant them with as little delay as possible into a bed which has been previously prepared. Plant them to a depth of 23cm(9in) and 45cm(18in) apart. Cover the crowns with 10cm(4in) of soil.

Cultivation Remove any weeds as soon as they appear. Cut back fern, after it has changed colour but before the plant seeds, to ground level. Dress the surface with manure or compost at the same time. Feed with liquid fertilizer in the early spring.

Pests and diseases Treat with derris in early summer to prevent attack from the asparagus beetle.

Harvesting Asparagus should not be harvested until it is in its third year growth. Cut the shoots when they are about 10cm(4in) in height. Use a sharp knife to make a clean cut about 5cm(2in) below the surface.

How to freeze

Preparation Remove woody ends, wash thoroughly and scrape to remove scales. Cut into even lengths and sort the spears into thick and thin stems.

Blanching Thin stems – 2 minutes.
　　　　　 Thick stems – 4 minutes.

Packing Use rigid containers.

Freezer life 9 months.

To use Either thaw overnight in the refrigerator or cook direct from the freezer in boiling water.

Above *Both fresh and frozen aubergine slices may be cooked and puréed to make an unusual vegetable dish.*

Aubergine

The aubergine or eggplant is a tropical plant which may also be grown in temperate climes in sheltered areas in the open, and under glass in areas which are exposed. Most varieties produce large purple fruit but there are also white varieties.

How to grow

Soil Most types.

Aspect Sunny and sheltered.

Sowing Sow during the autumn in tropical areas, late winter or spring elsewhere, but whether inside or outside, the temperature should not fall below 18°C(65°F). Prick out seedlings as soon as they are large enough to handle and, if growing inside, transfer them to 6cm(2.5in) pots and pot on finally into 18cm(7in) pots filled with potting compost.

Cultivation Water well and pinch out the tips to encourage lateral growth when the plants are about 15cm(6in) high. Help the flowers to set fruit by spraying them with water, especially if the weather is hot and dry. The plants will need the support of canes at this stage. Restrict the fruits to four to six per plant and feed the plants with weak liquid fertilizer at regular intervals.

Pests and diseases None to worry about.

Harvesting Gather the fruit when slightly soft.

How to freeze

Preparation Wash and cut into thick slices.

Blanching 4 minutes.

Packing Either open freeze and pack in plastic bags or pack in rigid containers with greaseproof paper between layers.

Freezer life 12 months.

To use Either thaw overnight in a refrigerator and fry, or cook direct from the freezer in boiling water.

17

Above *Easy to grow and good to eat, broad beans are an ideal vegetable for the home gardener. Try picking them before the beans have formed properly and cook and serve them in their shells.*

Beans, Broad

The broad bean is the hardiest member of the bean family. Like all pulses it is not only nutritious to eat, it also nourishes the soil by replacing nitrogen.

How to grow
Soil Most rich soils.
Aspect Not important.
Sowing Sow seeds in late winter in boxes or individual pots and start under glass. Prick out seedlings in early spring. Or sow outside as soon as the soil is soft enough to dig, in rows 75cm(2.5ft) apart, 5cm(2in) deep and 15cm(6in) apart. This will produce a later crop. Autumn sowing is possible in areas which can rely on mild winters.
Cultivation Provide the plants with some support in exposed gardens.
Pests and diseases Prevent blackfly by breaking off and removing the top 8cm(3in) of the plant as soon as the first pods have formed at the base. If it is too late, dust or spray with derris.
Harvesting Always pick while young, before they become starchy. Very tiny pods may be picked before the beans have formed properly and treated in the same way as mangetout, that is by cooking them in their shells and eating the entire pod.
How to freeze
Preparation Shell.
Blanching 2 minutes.
Packing Open freeze and pack in plastic bags.
Freezer life 12 months.
To use Cook direct from the freezer in boiling water.

Beans, Dwarf French

The French bean and the haricot are, in fact, different forms of the same plant. When the young whole bean, including the pod, is eaten, it is called the French bean. When the pod is discarded and only the ripe seeds are used, it is called the haricot. High in protein and vitamins and low in calories, it is an ideal vegetable for those on a diet.

How to grow
Soil Rich, light soils to which superphosphate of lime has been added at 90g(3oz) per sq m.(sq yd).
Sowing Do not sow until the soil is warm, that is, in late spring or early summer in temperate climes. Drills should be 45cm(18in) apart and the seeds sown at a depth of 3cm(1in) and 15cm(6in) apart in single or double rows.
Cultivation Water freely and mulch with peat in dry weather.
Pests and diseases None to worry about.
Harvesting Pick when the beans are no more than 10cm(4in) long, they taste better and are more tender. Avoid loosening the roots when picking. At the end of the season the plants may be allowed to ripen their remaining seeds in order to produce haricot beans. These can be used either as seeds for a new crop or for cooking. They last for as long as a year.
How to freeze
Preparation Wash, trim ends and remove any strings. Small beans may be frozen whole and larger beans sliced.
Blanching Whole – 3 minutes.
Sliced – 2 minutes.
Packing Open freeze and pack in plastic bags.
Freezer life 12 months.
To use Cook direct from the freezer in boiling water.

Beans, Runner

A native of tropical America, this plant will nevertheless thrive in cooler climates. At one time it was grown for the beauty of its bright scarlet blossoms alone.

How to grow
Soil Well cultivated, light soil to which compost has been added.
Aspect Sunny.
Sowing Either inside or under glass in spring, or outside in early summer when there is no risk of frost. This does not apply, obviously, to tropical zones. Sow outside 25cm(10in) apart and 5cm(2in) deep in double rows separated by a distance of at least 1.5m(5ft).
Cultivation Either support plants with stakes and string or netting to a height of about 2.4m(8ft) or convert into self-supporting bushes by continually pinching out the growing shoots. The latter method does not, however, produce such a good crop. Water frequently during dry periods, adding an occasional feed of liquid fertilizer. Spraying the plants when in flower will help them to set fruit.
Pests and diseases Protect plants sown outside from slugs by sprinkling slug pellets along the rows a week after sowing. Blackfly and greenfly can be controlled by watering and anti-aphid sprays.
Harvesting Pick frequently to encourage growth.
How to freeze
Preparation Wash, trim ends, and string if necessary. Cut into thick slices to preserve flavour and texture.
Blanching 2 minutes.
Packing Open freeze and put in plastic bags.
Freezer life 12 months.
To use Cook direct from the freezer in boiling water.

Top *By making time to water and feed a runner bean plant regularly, you will be rewarded by a heavy crop of tender beans.*

Above *Runner bean plants should either be supported with stakes or converted to self-supporting bushes by pruning. Staked plants give a higher yield.*

Left *French beans, picked when they are really young and tender, make a delicious salad, boiled, cooled and tossed in a vinaigrette sauce. The addition of thinly sliced strips of tomato will make a pleasing contrast in colour.*

Beetroot

This sweet salad vegetable has a high nutritional value. There are several different varieties varying in colour from red to gold to white and in shape from spherical to long and tapering. The round-shaped beetroot are easier to grow and taste and freeze better.

How to grow

Soil Light, rich, well-drained soil that has not been recently manured. Add a little sand to the soil as beetroot is a maritime plant.

Aspect Sunny and protected.

Sowing Sow seed from late spring to early summer when there is no danger of frost and the soil is warm. Sow fortnightly, as wanted through the summer, and into early autumn in mild temperate areas. Make drills 30cm(12in) apart and 3cm(1in) deep. Space seeds, which come in clusters, 10cm(4in) apart and thin to a final distance of 20cm(8in).

Cultivation Keep well watered as drought can cause bolting in the early stages and coarse, woody roots later. Keep weeds down by hand to avoid damaging the roots.

Pests and diseases None to worry about.

Harvesting Harvest when they are about the size of a golf ball. Take great care that neither the root nor the top growth are damaged when pulling them up. Remove leaves by carefully twisting them off but do not cut them as this causes the root to bleed and deteriorate in quality.

How to freeze

Preparation Wash and cook them until they are tender. Cool quickly in running water and rub off the skins. Leave small beetroots whole and dice or slice the larger ones.

Packing Pack in rigid containers.

Freezer life 6 months.

To use Thaw overnight in a refrigerator.

Below *Always remove beetroot by hand and not with a fork or spade. The leaves should be removed afterwards by carefully twisting them until they break off. These precautions are necessary in order to avoid any possibility of roots being cut and bleeding. Roots which bleed quickly deteriorate in flavour, texture and appearance.*

Right *Beetroots that have been harvested with care will be without blemish.*

Broccoli, Sprouting

Sprouting broccoli may be either purple, white or green, of which calabrese is the most tender form.

How to grow

Soil Firm, well-drained, medium to heavy soils. Prepare the autumn previous to sowing by forking in manure.

Aspect Sheltered.

Sowing From late spring to early summer in temperate climes; during the summer only in warmer climates. Sow in a long, thin line in drills 1cm(½in) deep and 23cm(9in) apart. Thin seedlings to 15cm(6in) apart as soon as they are large enough to handle. Plant out in summer leaving about 75cm(2.5ft) in both directions.

Cultivation Water the plants regularly until they are well established. Remove weeds by hand.

Pests and diseases Protect against the cabbage root maggot and club root by dipping the roots in a thin paste of four percent calomel dust and water when transplanting.

Harvesting Do not cut until the shoots are about 30cm(12in) long. Take centre spears first to encourage lateral growth.

How to freeze

Preparation Trim off outer leaves and any stems more than 3cm(1in) thick. Wash very thoroughly and cut into stems of even lengths.

Blanching Thin stems – 3 minutes.
Thick stems – 4 minutes.

Packing Open freeze and pack in rigid containers.

Freezer life 12 months.

To use Cook direct from the freezer in boiling water.

Brussels Sprouts

Cooked lightly in boiling water, Brussels sprouts are a delicious vegetable with a slightly nutty flavour. Unfortunately they only grow in temperate climates.

How to grow

Soil Rich, firm soil with natural or added lime, which has been well-manured for a previous crop.

Aspect Sheltered.

Sowing Sow seeds outside in early spring to a depth of 1cm($\frac{1}{2}$in) and keep adequately watered. Transplant in early summer when they have reached a height of about 15cm(6in). Allow 75cm(2.5ft) between both plants and rows; and firm well to ensure firm growth.

Cultivation Water young plants if the weather is hot and dry and hoe the soil frequently to keep down weeds. In exposed, windy areas it is advisable to stake plants in autumn. Remove yellow leaves as they appear.

Pests and diseases The same type and responding to the same treatment as for broccoli.

Harvesting Pick sprouts as they form from the base of the stem by pressing down and snapping them off. They are said to have a better flavour after a touch of frost. Do not remove the tops until the end of winter, but then, they too may be picked and used in the same way as cabbage.

How to freeze

Preparation Use only small, compact sprouts. Remove any discoloured leaves and wash thoroughly. Grade into sizes.

Blanching Small sprouts – 3 minutes.
Medium sprouts – 4 minutes.

Packing Open freeze and pack in plastic bags.

Freezer life 12 months.

To use Cook direct from the freezer in boiling water.

Cabbage

Cabbage can be divided into three main classes; spring cabbage, summer cabbage and winter cabbage which includes the savoy. By planting a combination of these it is possible to eat fresh cabbage throughout the year. Therefore it is only worth freezing cabbage if you only grow one of these varieties, have a glut or prefer red cabbage which has a much more limited season.

How to grow

Soil Firm, well-drained, medium to heavy soils to which a little lime and a lot of manure has been added. Do not add these together.

Aspect Sheltered.

Sowing Spring cabbage – sow thinly in drills in midsummer. Plant out in the autumn and firm well leaving 15cm(6in) between plants and

Above and left *Although it is possible to grow cabbages in succession throughout the year you may not wish to devote one section of your garden to a specific vegetable. Freezing them will give you a permanent supply of cabbage ready to use at a moment's notice.*

23

Above *A savoy or loose-headed cabbage. This is particularly good grilled whole and served with white sauce.*

Right *Both red and white cabbages taste especially good braised with apples. Fresh or frozen shredded cabbage may be used.*

45cm(18in) between the rows. Thin by removing alternate plants in late winter to use as spring greens.

Summer cabbage – Sow under glass in mid-winter or outside in spring. After hardening off, transplant in late spring.

Winter cabbage – sow in late spring and thin and plant out in midsummer.

All seedlings, no matter when planted, should be sown in shallow drills and watered in dry weather. In tropical areas sow cabbages from late summer to spring only, choosing small varieties.

Cultivation Transplanting should take place when the plants are about 10cm(4in) high, leaving lower leaves in the soil. Firm down the soil well in all cases and control weeds by hoeing. All cabbages benefit from feeds of liquid fertilizer and a dressing of 30g(1oz) of nitrogenous fertilizer per sq m(sq yd).

Pests and diseases The same type and responding to the same treatment as for broccoli. However, because of the high incidence of the cabbage root fly it is only advisable after such an attack to plant cabbages in the same area after a period of three years. Other pests may be prevented by spraying or dusting with derris and slugs are deterred by the lime dressing.

Harvesting Cut heads as soon as they are firm.

How to freeze

Preparation Wash thoroughly and shred.

Blanching $1\frac{1}{2}$ minutes.

Packing Pack in plastic bags and discard them after use as the smell lingers.

Freezer life 9 months.

To use Cook direct from the freezer in boiling water.

Carrots

There are so many varieties of carrot that it is possible to grow them throughout the year. It is, however, well worth freezing some both to be able to enjoy the flavour of tender carrots whenever you wish and also for convenience. The carrot is extremely versatile. It can be served on its own, as a soup, added to stews and used even in the preparation of cakes and jams. As all the vitamins are near to the surface, a carrot should ideally never be peeled but only lightly scraped. If the carrot is an old one, cook it first and then rub the

Left *Help keep the roots of carrots in perfect condition by never sowing them in soil that has been recently manured and by keeping them watered regularly in dry weather.*

Above *Although fresh or frozen baby carrots taste perfectly delicious on their own, try adding a sprinkling of aniseed to the cooking water for an interesting combination of flavours.*

skin off afterwards.

How to grow
Soil Light, well-drained and well-manured from a previous crop. Freshly manured soil causes root forking and excessive top growth.
Aspect Sunny and sheltered.
Sowing Sow under glass during the winter and outside throughout the rest of the year. Make drills 1cm($\frac{1}{2}$in) deep and 30cm(12in) apart. Sow very thinly as normal thinning makes them more vulnerable to attacks from the carrot fly.
Cultivation Always keep well-watered during dry weather to help prevent root-cracking. Hoe throughout the growing season to keep down weeds and keep the soil surface crumbly.
Pests and diseases The larva of the carrot fly, which is attracted by the smell of the leaves, can cause serious damage. Protect either by planting onions between the rows of carrots to mask their aroma or sprinkle with naphthalene at 30g(1oz) per 1m(1yd) of row. Prevent slugs by scattering slug pellets, and wireworms by dusting with lindane.

How to freeze
Preparation Slice off tops, wash well and scrape. If small, leave whole, otherwise slice or dice them.
Blanching Whole carrots – 3 minutes.
                 Diced or sliced carrots – 2 minutes.
Packing Open freeze and pack in plastic bags.
Freezer life 12 months.
To use Cook direct from the freezer in boiling water or hot melted butter.

Cauliflower

This delicious vegetable is reasonably easy to grow and freeze and will provide instant meals with the addition of cheese sauce. Unfortunately cauliflower is not suitable for growing in tropical climates.

How to grow

Soil Rich, deeply-dug soil with organic content to help water retention is essential. Add lime to acidic soils.

Aspect Sunny and open.

Sowing Sow under glass in late winter in seed compost and prick out to 5cm(2in) apart as soon as the seedlings are large enough to handle. Harden off outside in cold frames in early spring but protect from frosts. Alternatively, sow very thinly outside from spring onwards, in wide drills and transplant, leaving 45cm(18in) between both rows and plants.

Cultivation Firm soil well after transplanting. Keep well watered especially in dry weather. Hoe regularly to keep down weeds. As heads or curds appear protect any that are exposed by covering with a broken leaf, otherwise the sunlight will cause discoloration.

Pests and diseases See broccoli.

Harvesting Cut heads when mature, compact and white.

How to freeze

Preparation Strip off any leaves, wash thoroughly and either break into sprigs, or if small, leave whole.

Blanching Sprigs – 3 minutes.
             Whole – 4 minutes.

Packing Open freeze and pack in plastic bags.

Freezer life 6 months.

To use Cook direct from the freezer in boiling water.

Far left *Serve cauliflower with cheese sauce either as a side vegetable or as a light meal all on its own.*

Left *The cauliflower is a variety of cabbage which is cultivated for its undeveloped flower rather than its leaves. If you are cooking a whole head, leave a few of the tender, young leaves around the base as this both protects the head and adds to its appearance.*

Above *Unless there is danger of frost, celeriac is improved by drawing away the soil from the top of the root.*

Celeriac

The swollen, turnip-shaped roots of this vegetable do have a pronounced celery flavour. Celeriac may be eaten raw in salad or cooked in soups. Although it can be stored throughout the winter, it freezes well and is more accessible in this form.

How to grow

Soil Rich and heavy. Manure well in the autumn previous to sowing.

Aspect Not important.

Sowing Sow thinly in seed compost in a heated greenhouse at the beginning of spring in temperate climates, or outside in a sheltered place in warmer climates. Prick out into boxes of potting compost leaving 5cm(2in) between seedlings. Keep well watered. Harden off and plant out in early summer in rows 45cm(18in) apart leaving 30cm(12in) between plants. Plant so that the swollen root sits on the soil and maintain this throughout growth.

Cultivation As a celeriac root matures it may be necessary to draw soil away from it unless there is any danger of frost. Water copiously but carefully by spraying, and give weekly feeds of liquid fertilizer. Remove any side shoots and suckers from the root.

Pests and diseases None to worry about.

Harvesting Lift swollen roots carefully in late autumn.

How to freeze

Preparation Celeriac may be frozen either raw or puréed. Raw – wash, trim, scrape and cut into large slices or dice. Purée – peel, dice and simmer in stock or water using about ½litre (1pint) of liquid to 1kg(2lb) of celeriac, until all the liquid is absorbed. Either rub through a sieve or blend in a liquidizer to form a purée.

Blanching Raw celeriac should be blanched for 4 minutes.

Packing Raw – in rigid containers or plastic bags.
          Purée – in rigid containers.

Freezer life 6 months.

To use Raw – cook direct from the freezer in boiling water, or add direct to soups and stews, or thaw overnight and braise. Purée – heat in a pan with a little melted butter and seasoning for a vegetable, or thin with a little milk and serve as soup.

Celery

There are two basic varieties of celery, the self-blanching type and that which needs to be blanched by being earthed up. Celery that has been blanched has a little more flavour than the self-blanching variety but is less tender.

How to grow

Soil Slightly acidic soil which is rich in organic matter and is water retentive.

Aspect Not important.

Sowing Blanched celery should be sown under glass or in a protected corner in early spring in seed compost at a temperature of not less than 13°C(55°F). Sow very thinly and when the seedlings have developed a second leaf prick out into potting compost, leaving 5cm(2in) between each plant. Harden off in late spring and remember to keep adequately supplied with water. The seeds of self-blanching celery should be sown, thinned and hardened in the same way but about a month later in each case.

Cultivation In the previous autumn, prepare a trench for the blanched celery 60cm(2ft) wide and 30cm(12in) deep with equal amounts of soil on either side. Fork a 15cm(6in) layer of manure into the bottom of the trench, firm well and leave it to settle for as long as possible. In early summer transplant the seedlings to the trench leaving 30cm(12in) between each plant and flood the trench immediately afterwards to settle them. Keep plants well watered and feed occasionally with liquid fertilizer. When the plants are almost fully grown, remove any side shoots and low-growing leaves, tie the rest of the leaves loosely together and then earth them up until only a tuft of leaf is left growing on ridges. Self-blanching celery does not need this treatment and may be planted in flat ground leaving 23cm(9in) between plants each way and water them in.

Give both types plenty of water and weed regularly.

Pests and diseases Prevent or treat celery fly with derris/pyrethrum sprays.

Harvesting Blanched celery may be harvested about two months after earthing up but self-blanching varieties will be ready by mid-summer.

How to freeze

Preparation Use crisp, tender stalks only and remove any tough fibres. Wash thoroughly and cut into 5cm(2in) lengths.

Blanching 3 minutes.

Packing Pack in plastic bags.

Freezer life 9 months.

To use Celery should not be used raw after freezing, but is quite suitable to use as a cooked vegetable or in soups or stews.

Below left *Blanched celery should be planted in a trench with equal amounts of soil on either side. When the plant is almost mature, the leaves should be tied loosely together and the whole plant earthed up so that only the tops of the leaves remain on the surface.*

Below right *Celery that has been successfully blanched should have beautiful, white, crisp stems.*

Top *Although chicory is often used raw, chopped up and added to salads, it tastes equally good when boiled or braised.*

Above *Before using chicory, the outside leaves should be removed and the stalks trimmed.*

Chicory

Chicory provides a welcome contrast in texture to limp, winter lettuce. Its crispness and flavour make it an ideal salad vegetable raw, but it is equally good cooked.

How to grow

Soil Light, fertile, well-drained soils which are not acidic and have not been recently manured.

Aspect Not important.

Sowing Sow outside in early summer in drills 1cm($\frac{1}{2}$in) deep and 30cm(12in) apart. When the plants are about 5cm(2in) high, thin to 23cm(9in) apart in the rows.

Cultivation Keep free of weeds, and water during periods of dry weather. In late autumn, when the tops have begun to die down, carefully lift the roots. Cut back the top growth to the top of the root and trim off the ends of the roots. Discard any thin or fanged roots. Pack the prepared roots upright closely together in boxes or large clay flower pots filled with damp potting soil. Unless blanched in absolute darkness, the chicons, as the blanched roots are called, will be yellow and bitter. Cover with another box, pot or sheet of black plastic and leave in a frost-free area with a temperature of about 10°C(50°F) and every root will soon produce a chicon.

Pests and diseases None to worry about.

Harvesting When the chicons are 15cm(6in) tall, cut them off at soil level and discard the roots.

How to freeze

Preparation Remove any bruised outside leaves and trim the stalks.

Blanching 2 minutes.

Packing Drain thoroughly and pack in rigid containers or plastic bags.

Freezer life 9 months.

To use Chicory cannot be used raw in salads after freezing but will taste excellent cooked direct from the freezer, either in boiling stock or braised in a little butter.

Kale

Also known as borecole, this extremely hardy vegetable is particularly recommended to gardeners in very cold areas, as it will survive quite severe weather conditions. Although the leaves of kale cannot be used for this purpose after freezing, fresh, crisp leaves, washed and shredded, make an unusual addition to salads.

How to grow
Soil Will grow even in poor soils, although those which are particularly acidic or which have been manured recently are to be avoided.
Aspect Open.
Sowing Sow in spring in drills 15cm(6in) apart and 3cm(1in) deep. Transplant from midsummer onwards, leaving 45cm(18in) for dwarf varieties and 60cm(2ft) for taller ones, between each plant.
Cultivation Dress the surface of the bed, about one month after transplanting, with compost or manure. Draw soil from between the rows over the compost or manure to form a low ridge over the stems of the plants. Hoe regularly to keep down the weeds.
Pests and diseases Protect seedlings from the flea beetle by dusting with lindane.
Harvesting Plants should be beheaded reasonably early in the year to promote short side shoots. Leave large leaves as they tend to be bitter and pick only the small, young leaves.

How to freeze
Preparation Discard any leaves which are discoloured or coarse. Remove the young, tender leaves from the stems and wash thoroughly.
Blanching 2 minutes.
Packing Pack in plastic bags.
Freezer life 9 months.
To use Cook direct from the freezer in boiling water.

Kohlrabi

Kohlrabi is a root vegetable with a flavour similar to that of a turnip but more distinctive. It withstands dry soil conditions better than most vegetables.

How to grow
Soil Light, well-drained soils to which lime has been added.
Aspect Open.
Sowing Seeds can be sown thinly throughout spring and early summer in drills 3cm(1in) deep and 38cm(15in) apart. Thin seedlings gradually until they are 23cm(9in) apart as soon as they are large enough to handle. In areas with very mild winters, seeds may also be sown in the autumn.
Cultivation Kohlrabi matures quickly and needs little attention other than keeping down the weeds.
Pests and diseases Can suffer from club root. Treat in the same way as broccoli.
Harvesting Gather the green or purple 'roots' at the base of the stem when they are no larger than a cricket ball.

How to freeze
Preparation Cut off tops and scrub. Small kohlrabi may be left whole; older and larger specimens should be peeled and diced.
Blanching Whole – 3 minutes.
　　　　　　Diced – 2 minutes.
Packing Open freeze and pack in plastic bags.
Freezer life 12 months.
To use Cook direct from the freezer in boiling water.

Top *Although kale is a member of the cabbage family, its blue-green, curly leaves do not form a heart.*

Above *Always referred to as a root vegetable, the 'root' of kohlrabi which we eat actually grows above the ground.*

Leeks

The leek has the most subtle flavour of any member of the onion family. Because of its culinary value and the fact that it is not available throughout the year, the leek is well worth growing and freezing.

How to grow
Soil Almost any soil that does not become water-logged in winter.
Aspect Not important.
Sowing Sow outside in shallow drills during spring and early summer. Using a dibber, make a row of holes 15cm(6in) deep and 23cm(9in) apart. Drop the plants in the holes and fill with water which will wash sufficient soil down on to the roots.
Cultivation Water during dry weather and hoe regularly to keep the weeds down. Earth them up to blanch the stems. Give occasional feeds of liquid manure.
Pests and diseases Almost trouble-free. Water-logged conditions can lead to white rot. Protect from this and the onion fly with calomel dust.

Below *The leek is grown in earthed-up trenches in order to blanch the stems.*

Harvesting Lift as soon as the leeks are large enough to use.

How to freeze

Preparation Remove the coarse outer leaves and cut off the green tops. Wash thoroughly. Leave small leeks whole but slice thicker ones into 5 cm(2in) rings.

Blanching Whole – 4 minutes.

Sliced – 2 minutes.

Packing Pack in plastic bags or rigid containers.

Freezer life 6 months.

To use Add direct from the freezer to soups and stews or cook in boiling water.

Lettuce

Lettuce can be classified into three groups – cabbage, cos and loose-leaf. It cannot be frozen and thawed for use raw in salads because it has a high water content but it is worth freezing for cooking purposes. Varieties are being developed for garden use which will grow all the year round.

How to grow

Soil All varieties do better in moist, well-drained soil that has preferably been manured for a previous crop.

Aspect Sunny.

Sowing First sowings may be made under glass in late winter. The temperature of the greenhouse should be kept at 13–16°C(55–60°F). Sow thinly in shallow trays and prick off into deeper ones, spacing the seedlings at 5 cm(2in) intervals, as soon as they are large enough to handle. Harden off in a cold frame about four weeks later and plant out in spring. Plant in rows at 30cm(12in) intervals and protect with cloches if possible. Sow outside when the soil has warmed up, from early spring to midsummer, in 3cm(1in) deep drills spaced 38cm(15in) apart. Keep down weeds by hoeing and thin seedlings to a distance of 30cm(12in) when the lettuces have formed three or four leaves.

Cultivation Avoid overcrowding and keep adequately supplied with water or the lettuces will bolt.

Pests and diseases Protect seedlings from birds with strands of dark cotton stretched over the rows. Dust or spray with derris to deter

Above *Loose-leafed varieties of lettuce do not have to be completely removed when picking, just take off as many leaves as you require.*

Left *In order to promote firm hearts in cabbage lettuces, and to discourage them from bolting, they should be spaced well apart and watered regularly.*

Above *Cos, like most varieties of lettuce, is normally eaten raw as a salad. All lettuces, however, taste just as good either braised in butter or made into soup.*

Top right *All marrow and courgette plants have male and female flowers. For fruit to set the female flower must be pollinated by the male. As this is not always achieved by insects, it is advisable to do this by hand.*

Top far right *The courgette is not of a different species from the marrow but is only either the fruit of a special variety of small marrow or an ordinary marrow gathered when very young.*

Bottom right *Courgettes have a more distinctive flavour than marrows and may be cooked either by steaming, baking, deep-frying or sautéeing, as in this picture.*

or treat aphids.

Harvesting Cut as soon as the lettuces are firm and well-developed.

How to freeze

Preparation Remove coarse outer leaves and cut off root. Wash thoroughly and either separate into leaves or leave the hearts whole.

Blanching 2 minutes.

Packing Squeeze out moisture and pack in rigid containers.

Freezer life 6 months.

To use Either thaw overnight and braise or add direct from the freezer to soups.

Marrows and Courgettes

Courgettes, or zucchini as they are often called, are only either a special variety of small marrow or ordinary marrows gathered when very young.

How to grow

Soil Very rich, well-drained soil. A heap of well-rotted compost is the perfect site.

Aspect Sunny and sheltered.

Sowing Sow two seeds indoors in late spring per peat pot filled with seed compost and keep warm. Alternatively, sow outside in early summer by sowing three seeds at a time in the final cropping position and cover with a cloche or jam jar. Insert the seeds sideways to a depth of about 1cm($\frac{1}{2}$in). In both cases, thin seedlings to one strong plant. Do not transplant seedlings grown indoors, or remove cloches from those grown outside, until well into the summer when there is absolutely no risk of frost. Leave 1m(1yd) between bush varieties and 1.5m(5ft) between trailers.

Cultivation Watering during dry weather is essential. Weeding should also be done until the leaves are sufficiently large to shade the soil and inhibit their growth. All plants have male and female flowers. The female flower may be recognized by the embryo fruit behind the flower. The fruit will not set unless the female flower is pollinated. This is not always achieved by insects and hand pollination is often advisable. Pick a recently opened male flower, strip off the petals and push its stamens into the centre of the female flower.

Pests and diseases Scatter slug pellets to prevent slugs attacking seedlings.

Harvesting Cut courgettes as soon as they are about 8cm(3in) in length. If they are left to grow large, the plant will stop producing new flowers. Marrows also need cutting while they are still young and tender.

How to freeze

Preparation Marrows – young, tender marrows may be simply peeled and sliced, older marrows should be peeled, de-seeded, sliced, cooked until tender and puréed. Courgettes – wipe clean and cut into slices, and either leave raw or sauté in butter for one minute.

Blanching Marrows raw – 3 minutes.

Courgettes raw – 2 minutes.

Packing Marrows and courgettes – pack uncooked in plastic bags and sautéed or puréed in rigid containers.

Freezer life Marrows blanched – 10 months.

Marrows cooked – 6 months.

Courgettes – 12 months.

To use Thaw raw vegetables overnight in the refrigerator, reheat puréed marrow in melted butter. Finish cooking sautéed courgettes straight from the freezer in butter until golden brown and tender.

Onions

Onions for salad, that is spring onions or scallions, are grown from seed, and onions for cooking from either seed or sets. As spring onions do not freeze well and large cooking onions are available throughout the year, it is only really worth freezing small cooking onions, or pickling or pearl onions as they are also called.

How to grow

Soil Almost all soils.

Aspect Sunny and open.

Planting Sets are onions grown from seed the previous year. In the spring, push the sets into the soil so that the soil just covers them. Leave 15cm(6in) between plants and 30cm(12in) between rows.

Cultivation As they start to grow, scrape sufficient soil away from each plant to expose the top of the bulb. Weed regularly.

Pests and diseases Onions grown from sets are virtually trouble-free, except that they should be protected from birds until the green leaf tips begin to show when they lose interest.

Harvesting The onions are ready to harvest when the skins begin to turn yellow. Lift carefully and leave to dry upside down in the sun. If you want small onions, pull as soon as they are large enough to use.

How to freeze

Preparation Peel. Leave small onions whole but chop or slice large ones. Blanching is only necessary for long periods of storage.

Blanching 2 minutes.

Packing Pack in plastic bags and then overwrap to avoid cross-flavouring.

Freezer life Unblanched – 3 months.
 Blanched – 6 months.

To use Add whole or chopped onions to dishes while still frozen or cook gently in stock or butter.

Parsnips

Parsnips are a valuable fresh vegetable in winter, but taste so good that it is worth freezing some for the summer months.

How to grow
Soil Rich soil, well manured from a previous crop. Recently manured soil causes root forking.

Aspect Open.

Sowing Sow throughout the spring but choose a calm day to prevent the seeds from being blown away. Sow in 3cm(1in) deep drills at intervals of 10cm(4in), leaving 45cm(18in) between drills. Do not transplant as this will generally result in some injury to the tap root. Instead, thin seedlings when they are large enough to handle to 20cm(8in) apart.

Cultivation Needs little after-care other than hoeing to keep down weeds.

Pests and diseases Parsnips are susceptible to canker which appears as brown or black patches on the roots. There is no effective cure but the later you plant, the less risk there is.

Harvesting They are ready for lifting when the leaves begin to die off in the autumn. A better flavour is achieved, however, if they are left in the soil until they have been touched by frost, in areas where this is possible.

How to freeze
Preparation Scrub, trim and peel young parsnips. Cut into thin strips or dice.

Blanching 2 minutes.

Packing Open freeze and pack in plastic bags.

Freezer life 9 months.

To use Add direct from the freezer to soups and stews or cook as required.

Top left *Large onions should be chopped and sliced before freezing, but small onions may be frozen whole.*

Bottom left *As the onion begins to mature, the soil should be scraped away from the top of the bulb in order to expose it.*

Above *The root of the parsnip is slightly aromatic and has a sweet flavour.*

Above left *Supports for peas to grow up should be erected as soon as the seed is sown.*

Above right *Peas freeze particularly well, and whether you eat them straight from the garden or out of the freezer, the superiority in flavour of home-grown over commercially produced crops quickly becomes apparent.*

Peas and Mangetout

The garden or green pea is a highly nutritious legume widely grown as a farm crop and a popular vegetable in the garden. Peas can be divided into two groups, smooth (round-seeded) or wrinkled (marrow fats). The smooth variety is hardier but wrinkle-seeded have a finer flavour. Peas may be dwarf or tall and can be grown in succession over several months. Mangetout, or snow peas, are a variety of pea which is harvested before the pea is fully formed and the whole shell eaten.

How to grow
Soil Light, well-drained soils. Acidic or heavy clay soils are not suitable.
Aspect Protected.
Sowing Seed is sown in 5cm(2in) deep drills, 20cm(8in) apart. Sprinkle thinly into the drill so that each seed is about 8cm(3in) from the next. Should the soil be dry, the drill should be flooded with water and allowed to drain before sowing. Cover the seeds with soil raked over them. The distance between rows should be equal to the height of the variety being grown. Supports should be erected as soon as the seed is sown.
Cultivation Do not thin seedlings. Hand weed in order not to disturb the roots. For the same reason cut the tops off the weeds rather than uprooting them.
Pests and diseases Scatter slug pellets to protect seedlings from these predators. Spraying with nicotine solution will help protect the plants from the pea moth when the flowers are setting.
Harvesting Peas should be harvested before the pods become really tight and there is still some give in them. Try to cook or freeze them as soon as possible after picking as their flavour deteriorates rapidly.
How to freeze
Preparation Wash mangetout and leave whole. Pod peas.

Blanching 1 minute.
Packing Open freeze and put in plastic bags.
Freezer life 12 months.
To use Cook straight from the freezer in boiling water.

Peppers, Red and Green

A pepper becomes red or green depending upon how long the fruit is allowed to remain attached to the plant. A red pepper is simply more mature than a green one and not of a different variety. In temperate climes it is advisable, although not always necessary, to grow peppers inside. New varieties are being developed which will withstand somewhat colder weather.

How to grow
Soil Rich, light and moist.
Aspect Sunny and sheltered.
Sowing In most areas, sow indoors in early summer in a greenhouse or on a window sill, allowing two or three seeds per peat pot. In this way they can be transplanted without the roots being disturbed. When the seedlings are large enough to handle, transplant either to 20cm (8in) pots or into a greenhouse border leaving 60cm(2ft) between plants. Alternatively, transplant outside to organically rich soil and protect where necessary with cloches. In tropical areas, peppers can be sown outside in autumn or early winter.
Cultivation Wherever peppers are grown, they need regular watering in dry weather and weekly feeds of liquid manure. As they begin to produce fruit, their branches may need supporting. Cloches, where used, can be removed in midsummer.
Pests and diseases None to worry about.
Harvesting Peppers are worth picking as soon as they reach about 8cm(3in) in length. Leave the peppers to mature fully if you prefer the sweeter flavour of the red pepper.
How to freeze
Preparation Wash or wipe, cut off the stems and remove the seeds and membrane. Either leave whole or cut into halves, slices or dice.
Blanching Halved or whole – 3 minutes
                    Cut – 2 minutes.
Packing Pack into plastic bags or rigid containers.
Freezer life 12 months.
To use Thaw whole or halved peppers for three hours at room temperature. Sliced or diced peppers can be added to dishes straight from the freezer.

Above *To obtain the maximum growth from one plant, do not allow more than seven or eight peppers to mature at one time.*

Left *The red and green pepper are not different varieties of plant, as is often thought, but fruit from the same plant in different stages of maturity. The young pepper is always green, but gradually turns red as it ripens.*

Above *There are numerous varieties of potato, all subtly different in flavour. By growing your own, you can experiment with varieties of potato which are not normally available in the shops.*

Potatoes

All of the many varieties of potato fall into one of three groups – First Early, Second Early and Maincrop. This means that they are available throughout the year, so except for convenience, it is only really worth freezing new potatoes and those varieties which are good for chips, e.g. Majestic.

How to grow
Soil Light, rich soil, preferably lime-free and manured the autumn prior to planting.
Aspect Open and sunny.
Planting Potato plants are raised from seed tubers taken from the previous year's crop. Unpack tubers as soon as possible and place in trays in a light but frost-free room to sprout. This process is known as 'chitting' and results in an earlier crop. In frost-free areas plant in late winter to early spring, otherwise wait until the end of spring. Dig holes 13cm(5in) deep, 30cm(12in) apart in rows 60cm(2ft) apart, and drop the potatoes in, sprouts uppermost. In heavy soils, it is better to dig a trench to the same specifications and lay and cover the tubers more carefully to avoid breaking the shoots.
Cultivation Keep weeds down and, once the shoots are well through, earth up by drawing up the soil from between the rows around the plants, using a hoe. Continue to do this as they grow, as this prevents tubers from becoming exposed to the light and turning green.
Pests and diseases Prevent potato blight, which occurs in consistently wet weather, by dusting with Bordeaux powder. If the disease persists and the spotting on the leaves becomes black instead of brown,

then cut down and burn the foliage and lift the rest of the crop.

Harvesting Ascertain when the crop is ready by scraping away some of the earth, and lift the tubers as soon as they are large enough to eat.

How to freeze

Preparation Only new potatoes should be frozen uncooked.

Uncooked – wash and scrape.

Boiled – New potatoes only, which have been part-boiled, drained and tossed in butter may be left whole, otherwise they should be mashed with a little butter and milk or made into croquettes or duchesse potatoes.

Roast – cook until tender but not crisp and drain on absorbent paper.

Chipped – Fry for about 2 minutes in clean oil until soft but not coloured. Drain on absorbent paper.

Baked – Remove pulp, mash with butter and return to their shells.

Blanching Uncooked new potatoes – 4 minutes.

Packing Uncooked – in plastic bags or preferably in boiling bags with a knob of butter.

Boiled – Cool and pack in plastic bags or preferably in boiling bags with a knob of butter.

Mashed – Cool and pack in boiling bags.

Croquettes and duchesse – open freeze and pack in plastic bags or rigid containers.

Roast – Cool, open freeze and pack in rigid containers.

Chipped – Open freeze and pack in plastic bags.

Baked – Wrap in foil.

Freezer life Uncooked – 12 months.

             Chipped – 6 months.

             All other cooked potatoes – 3 months.

To use

Uncooked – cook direct from the freezer, in boiling bags where used, in boiling water.

Boiled – thaw loose potatoes and reheat in melted butter or, if in boiling bags, reheat in boiling water.

Mashed – reheat direct from the freezer by dropping the sealed bag in boiling water.

Croquettes – fry direct from the freezer for 6 minutes.

Duchesse – bake direct from the freezer at 400°F(Gas Mark 6, 200°C) for 30 minutes.

Roast – reheat in the oven direct from the freezer adding a little fat or oil if necessary, at 400°F (Gas Mark 6, 200°C), for 30 minutes.

Chipped – deep fry direct from the freezer to deep golden brown but beware – they will spit a lot.

Baked – leave in their foil and reheat in the oven for 30 minutes at 400°F(Gas Mark 6, 200°C).

Top left *In order to promote early growth, seed tubers are exposed and left to sprout before planting.*

Top centre *Plant seed tubers which have been 'chitted' so that the sprout is uppermost.*

Top right *Once the shoots have come through, the soil from between the rows should be drawn up to the plants in order to blanch them.*

Above *An alternative way to blanch potatoes, other than by earthing them up, is to cover the newly planted tubers with a sheet of black plastic. Holes should be made in the plastic in order for the shoots to develop.*

Pumpkin

From the same family as the marrow, the pumpkin is grown and used in much the same way.

How to grow
Soil Very rich, preferably on a compost heap.
Aspect Sunny and protected.
Sowing Sow in pots under glass in spring. In colder areas slight heat may be necessary for germination. Thin seedlings to leave one in each pot and harden them off for setting outside in early summer. Alternatively, sow outside in early summer, under cloches in temperate climes. In either case, leave 1m(1yd) between plants and lots of room on either side as main shoots can attain a final length of 3.5m (4yds).
Cultivation Control spread of main shoots by pinning them to the ground with pieces of soft wire bent to the shape of a hairpin. If the female flowers do not set they should be hand pollinated in the same way as the marrow. Water regularly in dry weather. As soon as the small fruits begin to swell, give feeds of liquid manure. Stop this when the fruits have reached a desirable size and leave to ripen.
Pests and diseases Prevent slugs by scattering slug pellets.
Harvesting Harvest as soon as they are large enough to cook.
How to freeze
Preparation Wash, peel, halve and remove seeds and string. Cut into slices or dice and steam or boil until tender and then mash.
Packing Cool and pack in rigid containers or boiling bags.
Freezer life 12 months.
To use Either reheat direct from the freezer in the top of a double boiler or drop boiling bags in boiling water and reheat. Alternatively, thaw overnight in the refrigerator and use for pies and soups.

Top *Keep a supply of frozen puréed pumpkin in order to be able to make tasty pies and soups throughout the year.*

Above *Pumpkins can grow to an enormous size but need a very rich soil in order to do so. A compost heap is the ideal planting site. If the pulp is removed with care, the shells can be used to make lanterns.*

Salsify

Also known as the vegetable oyster because of its delicate flavour, salsify is a root vegetable much appreciated by gourmets. There are two types of salsify, one with white roots and one with black. The latter is said to have the better flavour and is also called scorzonera.

How to grow

Soil Light and manured from a previous crop. Recent manuring causes root forking.

Aspect Open.

Sowing Sow thinly in 3cm(1in) deep drills in late spring. Leave 38cm(15in) between rows and thin seedlings as soon as they are large enough to handle to 30cm(12in) apart.

Cultivation Salsify needs very little attention as it is reasonably hardy. The scorzonera variety may be left in the ground until the following year.

Harvesting Great care must be taken when lifting, as damaged roots are liable to bleed and this impairs the flavour.

How to freeze

Preparation Trim and scrub but do not peel.

Blanching 2 minutes, then peel while still warm.

Packing Cool and cut into 8cm(3in) lengths and pack in plastic bags.

Freezer life 12 months.

To use Cook direct from the freezer in boiling water and serve tossed in butter or in a white sauce.

Below *Fresh salsify tastes superb sautéed in a little butter and sprinkled with parsley.*

Seakale Beet

Not as well known as it deserves to be, this vegetable, also known as Swiss chard, is dual purpose. Although it is a form of beet, there is no edible root. Instead it produces large glossy leaves, which are cooked like spinach, from which the mid-ribs are removed and cooked like celery.

How to grow
Soil Most soils but preferably rich.
Aspect Sheltered.
Sowing Sow thinly in spring in drills 3cm(1in) deep and 38cm(15in) apart. Thin seedlings when quite small to 23cm(9in) apart.
Cultivation Except for hoeing, weeding and possibly mulching, the plants need almost no attention. In very dry weather they benefit from watering. By spreading a light covering of straw over the bed in autumn the plant will continue producing leaves throughout the winter and into the following spring. In mild climates this covering is unnecessary.
Pests and diseases Virtually trouble free.
Harvesting Pull regularly but do not strip all of the leaves from any one plant when picking. Pick by twisting the leaves away from the base rather than cutting.

How to freeze
Preparation Wash thoroughly and strip off the green part of the leaf from the mid-ribs and keep separate. Slice the mid-ribs into 5cm(2in) lengths.
Blanching Leaves – 2 minutes. Mid-ribs – 3 minutes.
Packing Pack separately in plastic bags or rigid containers.
Freezer life 12 months.
To use Cook direct from the freezer in boiling water.

Spinach

There are four types of spinach; summer spinach, winter spinach, perpetual or spinach beet and New Zealand spinach. Botanically they are quite different but what they do have in common is appearance, flavour and a high nutritive value of vitamins and minerals.

How to grow
Soil Summer – rich, moisture-retaining and well dug.
Winter and perpetual – any soil that does not become waterlogged. New Zealand – will grow even in poor dry soil if watered and manured.
Aspect Summer – shady.
Winter, perpetual, New Zealand – sheltered and sunny.
Sowing Sow summer spinach from early spring to midsummer for a continuous supply. Seeds should be sown thinly in drills 3cm(1in) deep and 30cm(1ft) apart. Thin the seedlings to 8cm(3in) as early as possible.

Sow winter spinach from midsummer to mid-autumn. Thin seedlings to 15cm(6in) apart. Give protection from frosts where necessary with cloches or straw.

Perpetual spinach may be sown throughout the summer. Germination is accelerated by soaking the seeds overnight before sowing. Keep the ground moist until the seedlings appear. Leave 45cm(18in) between drills and thin seedlings to 23cm(9in) apart.

Sow New Zealand spinach under glass in spring, or outside in early summer. Sow very thinly in drills 1m(1yd) apart. Thin seedlings to 60cm(2ft) apart.

Top *Both the stem and leaf of seakale beet may be eaten. Each is cooked differently and have distinct but excellent flavours.*

Above *New Zealand spinach tastes delicious and has a high nutritional value.*

Cultivation This consists of regular hoeing to keep down weeds. Mulching with peat or straw will reduce this work. Always keep spinach well watered during dry weather, particularly summer spinach.

Pests and diseases Yellowing of leaves is caused by spinach blight. When it is apparent, destroy leaves immediately and do not grow in the same area for several years. Spinach blight is very rare.

Harvesting Start as soon as the leaves are of usable size, do not wait until they become tough. Regular picking promotes growth but do not completely strip the plant.

How to freeze

Preparation Remove the stems and any bruised or discoloured leaves. Wash thoroughly and strip leaves off stalks. Either keep the leaves whole and freeze uncooked, or chop and cook, without adding any water, until tender.

Blanching Uncooked – 2 minutes.

Packing Pack both cooked and uncooked spinach in plastic bags or rigid containers.

Freezer life 12 months.

To use Cook raw spinach direct from the freezer in a little butter. Reheat cooked spinach direct from the freezer in the top of a double boiler and add seasoning, butter and a little cream.

Below *All varieties of spinach make delicious soup. If you have the time, the soup may be prepared and frozen for later use. Do not add cream or garnishes until after the soup has been thawed and reheated.*

Swedes

The swede is related to the turnip but is a little larger and has a slightly sweeter flavour.

How to grow
Soil Rich and well manured from a previous crop.
Aspect Open and sunny.
Sowing Sow very thinly in early summer in 3cm(1in) deep drills at 38cm(15in) intervals. Thin the seedlings to 30cm(12in) apart as soon as they are large enough to handle.
Cultivation If growth appears rather slow, topdress and hoe into the ground nitrate of soda at the rate of 30g(1oz) to a row of 3m(10ft). This fertilizer, or another nitrogenous fertilizer, should be watered in if the weather is consistently dry. Hoe to keep down the weeds or mulch with peat or chopped straw.
Pests and diseases Prone to the same problems and responds to the same treatment as cabbage.
Harvesting Allow to mature fully before lifting.
How to freeze
Preparation Peel and cut into slices or dice.
Blanching 3 minutes.
Packing Pack into plastic bags or rigid containers.
Freezer life 12 months.
To use Cook direct from the freezer in boiling water.

Sweetcorn

Sweetcorn is a native of America and, although a cereal, is treated as a vegetable.

How to grow
Soil Well dug and dressed with compost.

Right *Swedes are traditionally eaten cooked in stews and casseroles or as a puréed vegetable. Try serving your fresh or frozen swedes with cheese sauce for an unusual variation.*

46

Left *The difference in flavour between a fresh corn-on-the-cob, whether it is boiled, steamed or baked, and the canned variety is usually only a treat to be enjoyed for a few weeks in the autumn. By growing and freezing your own sweetcorn you can enjoy them throughout the year.*

Aspect Sunny and protected from strong winds and frosts.

Sowing In temperate, cooler climes, sow two or three seeds in 8cm(3in) pots in a cold frame or under a cloche in early summer. Thin seedlings to one strong plant in each pot. Set the plants outside when there is absolutely no danger of frost. In warmer areas, sow outside in late spring, in 3cm(1in) deep drills, 38cm(15in) apart. In tropical areas, sowing can go on through into autumn. Several short rows are preferable to one or two long ones as this helps wind pollination. Pollination is effected by the wind blowing pollen from the male tassels on the top of the plant on to the female part of the cob, or silk, which lies between the leaf and stem. Obviously, the more compactly they are grown the higher the chances of fertilization.

Cultivation In dry summers, water as necessary. Feed the plants with liquid manure if the soil is not very good. Hand weed to protect the shallow roots, or mulch in midsummer.

Pests and diseases None to worry about.

Harvesting Harvest when the silks which hang from the top are black-brown in colour and brittle. Check on maturity by carefully opening the top of the green sheath and pressing a grain with a finger nail. If a watery juice exudes, the cob is too young, if the grain contains paste it is too old, when it is perfectly ripe it should spurt a creamy liquid. Remove by twisting the cob off the plant. Freeze or cook as soon as possible after harvesting or the liquid sugar in the grains will convert to thick starch.

How to freeze

Preparation Strip off the leaves and silk threads, cut off the stems and grade for size. Alternatively, scrape off the kernels.

Blanching Small – 4 minutes.

Medium – 6 minutes.

Large – 8 minutes.

Packing Pack whole cobs in plastic bags. Kernels should be open frozen and then packed in rigid containers.

Freezer life 12 months.

To use Thaw whole cobs overnight in the refrigerator and cook in boiling water. Kernels should be cooked direct from the freezer in boiling water.

Above *Originally from South America, the tomato may be red or yellow in colour and round, oval or pear-shaped in appearance.*

Tomato

Although tomatoes may be grown inside or outside according to the variety and prevailing weather conditions, their season is limited and surplus produce is well worth freezing for cooking. Botanically a fruit, the tomato is nevertheless treated as a vegetable.

How to grow

Soil Well dug and dressed with manure or compost.

Aspect Very sunny, frost-free, and facing towards the sun.

Sowing Sow indoors in a temperature of about 16°C(60°F) in spring and prick off seedlings into 8cm(3in) pots when the first two leaves of the plant have folded back. Move to an unheated greenhouse in early summer and gradually, if desired, to a cloche and finally outside if the temperature does not fall below 10°C(50°F). In warmer climates, plants will need a little protection. Frost will kill a tomato plant, indeed any sudden change of temperature will affect the plant adversely. Before planting fill holes with water and wait for them to drain. Leave at least 1m(1yd) all round bush varieties and 60cm(2ft) around dwarf varieties.

Cultivation Plants should be supported by canes, stakes or a wire trellis. The plants need tying in regularly to the supports. Remove any side shoots in trained plants which develop between the leaf and stem. Weeds must be controlled. Once the first fruits have set, give a diluted feed with liquid fertilizer for tomatoes about once a week. For late-ripening varieties only, in the autumn, untie them and lower them on to clean straw to hasten ripening. Set cloches over them and leave the fruit to mature.

Pests and diseases Control whitefly by spraying with resmethrin.

Harvesting All fruit must be picked before the first frost. Pick as they ripen and place those which are not ready by late autumn in a drawer in a warm room to ripen.

How to freeze

Preparation Frozen tomatoes cannot be used for salads as they turn to pulp when thawed, because of their high water content. They may be frozen uncooked, whole or halved, or in the form of juice or purée. Whole or halved – wipe and remove stems and cut in half if large. Puréed – wipe, chop roughly, simmer in their own juice until soft and rub through a sieve or strainer.

Juice – chop, sieve or strain, or blend in a liquidizer and strain.

Blanching Uncooked – 2 seconds.

Packing Uncooked – open freeze and pack in plastic bags or rigid containers.

Juice or purée – pack in rigid containers.

Freezer life 12 months.

To use Whole – add to stews, soups, etc., direct from the freezer.

Halves – grill or fry direct from the freezer.

Juice – thaw overnight in the refrigerator, season.

Purée – thaw overnight in the refrigerator and use as required for soups, sauces, etc.

Turnip

A root vegetable which has been grown and eaten, at least in Britain, for many centuries. The roots are spherical or flat and round, and have a slightly nutty flavour.

How to grow

Soil Well-drained, medium loam ideally, but will grow in heavier soils. The soil should have been manured from a previous crop, but

not recently as this tends to cause excessive top growth and root forking. A little lime should be added if the soil does not contain any naturally.

Aspect Open.

Sowing The first sowing of summer turnips should be in early spring, followed by a second sowing in early summer. Sow thinly in 1cm(½in) deep drills 30cm(12in) apart. Thin seedlings to 10cm(4in) apart when large enough to handle. Winter turnips should be sown towards the end of summer or in autumn. Water drills if they are dry and leave to drain before sowing. Thin seedlings to 23cm(9in) apart as soon as they are large enough to handle.

Cultivation Hoe to keep down weeds and water regularly in dry weather. Winter varieties may need cloches to protect them from frost.

Pests and diseases Dust seedlings with derris to control flea beetles.

Harvesting Start pulling as soon as the turnips are large enough to use. If left to age they become coarse and fibrous and are only suitable for making soup.

How to freeze

Preparation Trim and peel. Small turnips may be left whole while larger ones should be cut into dice. Alternatively, simmer until tender and mash to a purée.

Blanching Whole – 4 minutes.
             Diced – 2 minutes.

Packing Pack raw turnips in plastic bags and puréed in rigid containers.

Freezer life 12 months.

To use Cook raw turnips straight from the freezer in boiling water. Puréed turnips should be reheated in the top of a double boiler. If you wish to roast them, thaw completely beforehand.

Top *Tomatoes that have been frozen are not suitable for eating raw. They are, however, fine for cooking and making soups.*

Above *Cooked like spinach, turnip leaves are as good to eat as the roots.*

Something to savour

Growing and using herbs is an enjoyable and rewarding pastime. Herbs both look and smell attractive and are virtually indispensable in the kitchen where their use helps to counter the general blandness of mass-produced food.

A herb is a plant which does not develop wood and of which the leaves, flowers or stems are used for culinary or medicinal purposes. Although there are literally thousands of different kinds of herbs grown throughout the world, only the few which have particular culinary merit and which respond well to freezing have been included. Freezing is particularly suited to those herbs which either do not appear, or die completely, in winter and do not dry well. This means, for instance, that you can enjoy the sight and flavour of freshly-chopped chives sprinkled over your food throughout the year, instead of using dried chives which smell and taste like old grass.

How to grow

The majority of herbs grow better in the open ground, but will also, with one or two exceptions, flourish in pots and tubs. Although some herbs are classified as perennials in their country of origin, they will not often survive a winter with frosts. Most herbs can be grown from seed. However, if you wish to be able to use them as soon as possible, it is probably more satisfactory to buy small plants and transplant them to your garden.

Although the individual conditions and advice relating to each herb are given separately, here are a few general points of information.

Soil Herbs will survive in most ordinary soils but tend to prefer those which are well-drained and slightly alkaline.

Planting Whether of seeds or plants, this should take place in spring, unless you wish to keep them in a container, and, in the case of seedlings, these should be thinned out to the distance recommended in the individual instructions. If you are planting in the open ground the soil should first have been dug over and levelled. In the case of pots and tubs a firm, moist compost is preferable. Seeds which are grown in boxes under glass should be kept warm and away from the light in order to provide the best conditions for germination.

Watering This obviously varies according to the individual requirements of each plant and prevailing weather conditions.

Pests Avoid spraying herbs with pesticides unless necessary. Greenfly can be a problem in the garden. A spray or dust with derris or pyrethrum, which are pesticides but very safe ones, will prevent or cure this problem. Plants under or behind glass are prone to whitefly. These resemble tiny flecks of ash or cotton and should either be be picked off by hand or removed with a matchstick which has been wrapped in cotton wool soaked in methylated spirit.

Harvesting All herbs should be picked in their prime but before they begin to flower. Gather them in the early morning before the sun reaches them and cut them with a sharp knife, except for chives, which should be cut with scissors.

Right *With their attractive appearance and aromatic leaves, herbs are as much an asset in the garden as they are in the kitchen.*

How to freeze

There are two basic methods of freezing herbs, either whole or chopped. Always freeze in small quantities.

Preparation Wash and then shake the herbs dry. There is no need to blanch them. Whole – separate them into small bunches. To make a bouquet garni, place together a sprig of thyme, parsley, any other herb you may wish to include, and a bay leaf. Tie them up with white thread and remember to leave a long tie so that they are easy to extract before serving – otherwise an unsuspecting guest may get an unpleasant shock! Chopped – chop the herbs up finely with a sharp knife or a pair of scissors.

Packaging Whole – pack the bunches either in foil or plastic bags. Seal and freeze. Chopped – pack the herbs tightly into an ice-cube tray and top up with water and freeze. Alternatively you could use the same principle but liquidize the herbs in a blender first. When the cubes are solid, turn them out into a plastic bag.

In both cases make sure the wrapping has been previously labelled.

Freezer life 6 months.

To use Bouquet garni and whole leaves may be used straight from the freezer. If you wish to chop whole leaves, this can be done by simply crumbling the leaf while it is still frozen. Chopped or blended herbs in cubes may also be used straight from the freezer, or if you prefer, the cubes of chopped leaves may be left to thaw in a fine strainer.

Balm *melissa officinalis*

Perennial

Better known as lemon balm, this herb has a delightful scent which attracts bees. It has heart-shaped leaves and small, whitish flowers.

Soil type Most soils providing that they are moist.
Aspect Sunny.
Height 60cm(2ft).
Planting Sow seeds in spring or buy one plant.
Distance between plants 1m(1yd).
Pot growth It is advisable to transplant to open ground unless you have a very large tub.
Propagation Either by root division in spring or autumn, or allow it to seed itself.
Remarks Great colonizer with fast-spreading roots.
Culinary use Herbal tea and stewed with fruit.

Below left *Use the leaves of balm as a substitute for lemon rind in savoury dishes.*

Below right *To make a bouquet garni, place together a sprig of thyme and parsley and a bay leaf. Wrap the herbs in a small square of cheesecloth and secure with white thread.*

Top right *Sprinkle chopped basil over sliced, raw tomatoes for a refreshing summer salad.*

Centre right *Chervil has a slight flavour of aniseed which tastes excellent with egg dishes and cheese sauces.*

Bottom right *Chives can be used to add a delicate oniony flavour to most vegetable salads.*

Basil *ocimum basilicum*
Annual

Originating from India, basil is a delicate plant. There are two basic varieties, sweet basil and bush basil. Sweet basil is larger, more aromatic and subtler in flavour than bush basil.

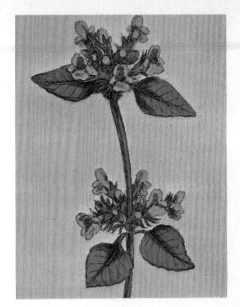

Soil type Light but rich.
Aspect Full sun.
Height 1m(1yd).
Planting Sow seeds in early summer. They should be grown in sterilized soil as they are prone to 'damping off' disease. Keep seedlings warm and protected. When planting seedlings out or inserting small bought, container grown plants, do so in a sheltered border.
Distance between plants 45cm(18in).
Pot growth Basil grows better in temperate climes when kept in pots in a greenhouse or conservatory. Pot diameter 35cm(14in).
Remarks Pinch out growing shoots to retard flowering and develop a leafy, bushy plant.
Culinary use Usually associated with tomatoes, both raw and cooked, particularly in the form of salads and soups. Equally good with egg dishes and on pizzas.

Chervil *anthriscus cerefolium*
Annual

Similar in appearance to parsley but more delicate and fern-like. It has a slight flavour of aniseed.

Soil type Most soils providing that they are moist.
Aspect Semi-shade.
Height 45cm(18in).
Planting Sow at intervals during the spring and summer.
Distance between plants 30cm(1ft).
Pot growth Grow in pots or window boxes. Ultimate pot diameter 12cm(5in).
Remarks Pinch out flower buds as soon as they appear as they retard leaf development.
Culinary use In soups, egg dishes, fish sauces and salads.

Chives *allium schoenoprasum*
Perennial

A member of the onion family and not strictly speaking a herb. It produces clumps of grass-like green spears and pretty mauvey-blue flowers.

Soil type Rich, slightly alkaline soils which are moist.
Aspect Shady.
Height 25cm(10in).
Planting Easily grown from seed sown in spring or early summer.
Distance between plants 23cm(9in).
Pot growth Will grow well in pots, needing one with a diameter of 18cm(7in).
Propagation Multiplies rapidly underground. Every three to four years divide during the autumn into clumps of about six bulblets and replant.
Remarks Do not allow flowers to develop as this means the stems thrive at the expense of the leaves. Cut clumps in rotation to about

Below *Dill has a delicate, feathery appearance and is unusual in that both the seeds and leaves are used in cooking.*

Bottom *Fennel has quite a strong aniseed flavour, so use sparingly.*

3cm(1in) above soil level, using a pair of scissors. This·will ensure a constant supply.

Culinary use Wherever a mild oniony taste is required, on salads, in cheese or egg dishes and over soups and cooked vegetables, especially new and jacket potatoes.

Dill *peucedanum graveolens*
Annual

Dill resembles the herb fennel in appearance, as it has delicate feathery leaves, but it does not share the same aniseed flavour.

Soil type Light.
Aspect Sunny.
Height 1m(1yd).
Planting Seeds may be grown either in pots or sown directly into the ground. Sow at intervals throughout the spring and summer.
Distance between plants 30cm(12in).
Pot growth Dill will grow in pots, if they are large and deep, but grows better in the open ground.
Remarks Dill water has been used for centuries to 'wind' babies.
Culinary use Both the leaves and seeds are used to flavour vinegar. Dill tastes particularly good in fish sauces, soups and with courgettes, pickled cucumbers and cabbage.

Fennel *foeniculum vulgare*
Perennial

Fennel is one of the earliest known herbs, and is recognized by its tall feathery leaves. It is said to stimulate the appetite and aid digestion.

Soil type Well-drained.
Aspect Sunny.
Height 1.5m(5ft).
Planting Sow seeds in spring or buy small plants.
Distance between plants 38cm(15in).
Pot growth Will grow in a pot or tub with a diameter of 18cm(7in).
Remarks Pinch out flowers on appearance. Better to plant at the back of the garden because of its height.
Culinary use Particularly good with fish and accompanying sauces; also with chicken and pork. Use sparingly.

Marjoram *pot marjoram: origanum onites*
oregano: origanum vulgare
sweet marjoram: origanum marjorana
Perennial
There are many varieties of marjoram, each with the same characteristic scent and flavour.

Soil type Well-drained, slightly acidic.
Aspect Full sun.
Height 60cm(2ft).
Planting All varieties can be grown from seed sown in spring in boxes. Do not sow outside until early summer.
Distance between plants 23cm(9in).
Pot growth Will grow in pots needing an ultimate pot diameter of 20cm(8in).
Remarks Cut regularly to encourage growth. Only pot marjoram can really be regarded as a perennial in cooler climates, where it is safer to treat other varieties as half hardy annuals.
Culinary use Most Italian dishes, particularly pizzas, and in stuffings, sausage meats and omelettes.

Mint *Spearmint: mentha spicata*
Applemint: mentha rotundifolia
Perennial
There are over 40 varieties of mint, all edible, of which spearmint, with its narrow, thin-textured leaf, and applemint, with a broader, fleshier and slightly hairy leaf, are the most common.

Soil type Most soils providing they are moist.
Aspect Sun or partial shade.
Height Spearmint 60cm(2ft), applemint 1m(1yd).
Planting Mint cannot be sown by seed but is grown from runners with good roots attached. Plant all varieties in spring or autumn.
Distance between plants One plant is all you need.
Pot growth Will grow in pots but keep plants pinched down to about 15cm(6in).
Propagation Cut roots into 15cm(6in) lengths and replant in spring or autumn.
Remarks All mints spread, restrain by planting roots in a container such as a bottomless bucket or by driving slates around it. Pinch out flower buds on appearance in order to maintain maximum leaf growth.
Culinary use Best known in the form of mint sauce or jelly served with meat, especially lamb. Also good with new potatoes and chopped and sprinkled over salads, particularly cucumber. Mint teas.

Below *There are many varieties of marjoram, including oregano, but each has the same characteristic scent and flavour. Whichever variety you use, marjoram tastes particularly good with Italian dishes.*

Bottom *Mint is usually associated with roast lamb and new potatoes. Try using it with sliced cucumbers and sour cream to make an unusual side salad.*

Top *Chopped parsley, judiciously sprinkled, complements most savoury dishes.*

Centre *The succulent leaves of the edible varieties of purslane make a refreshing addition to a green salad.*

Bottom *Rosemary is recommended to the gardener not only for its culinary value, but also for the smell of its aromatic leaves and the beauty of its blue-mauve flowers in the spring.*

Parsley *carum petroselinum*
Biennial

It is not surprising that parsley has been in use for over 3000 years as not only does parsley improve the taste and appearance of most dishes, but it is also rich in iron and vitamin C.

Soil type Moist but well-drained with natural or added lime.
Aspect Semi-shade.
Height 30cm(12in).
Planting Sow seeds from spring to mid-summer in drills 30cm(12in) apart. They take a long while to germinate in the open ground so it is easier to buy small plants.
Distance between plants 23cm(9in).
Pot growth Will grow in pots but they must be deep, or plant several in a large tub.
Remarks Pinch out flower buds, unless you want some to sow seed, and protect outdoor plants from severe frosts. Beware of poisonous fool's parsley springing up, although this does not present a great danger as it can be easily detected by its unpleasant smell.
Culinary use In parsley sauce and butter, and chopped and sprinkled over practically every savoury dish in the recipe book.

Purslane *portulaca oleracea*
Annual

An unusual herb with a distinctive flavour.

Soil type Dry and warm.
Aspect Sunny.
Height 15cm(6in).
Planting Sow seeds in spring and throughout summer.
Distance between plants Thin seedlings until the leaves of one plant can only just touch those of its neighbour.
Remarks Tends to spread in all directions.
Culinary use The young leaves may be used as a salad, but as it becomes older and more fibrous use the leaves in the same way as those of spinach, in soup and as a vegetable.

Rosemary *rosmarinus officinalis*
Perennial

The rosemary plant can live for 20 years or more and is worth cultivating for the smell of its aromatic leaves alone. It has pretty blue-mauve flowers in spring.

Soil type Sandy and well-drained.
Aspect Sunny.
Height 1.2m(4ft).
Planting Can be grown from seed sown in boxes in the early summer. Simpler and quicker to grow from rooted cuttings or bought plants.
Distance between plants 38cm(15in).
Pot growth Will grow in pots, needing an ultimate pot diameter of 35cm(14in).
Propagation Take cuttings in spring or after flowering and, when rooted, plant out the following autumn.
Remarks Will not tolerate permanently wet roots in winter, protect it also from frost.
Culinary use On roast meats, particularly lamb, with poultry dishes and in stuffings. Use sparingly.

Sage *salvia officinalis*
Perennial

This fast-spreading plant has had a reputation for centuries as a cure for all ills and an aid to longevity. It was much used by the Chinese, Greeks and Romans, who credited it with being good for the brain, the senses and the memory. The one fact that is known for certain, is that it is particularly good with rich, fatty meats as its strong flavour helps to counteract any greasiness.

Soil type Most soils if they are well-drained.
Aspect Full sun.
Height 60cm(2ft).
Planting The broad-leafed variety does not flower in cooler climates and must be bought as a plant or grown from cuttings, divisions or layers. Other varieties which have seeds should be sown in early summer in boxes and allowed to mature before being finally trans-planted.
Distance between plants 60cm(2ft).
Pot growth Will grow in a pot but this must be large.
Propagation For layers, peg down peripheral stems, and when they have grown independent roots, cut away and transplant.
Remarks Plant it at the back of the garden as it spreads quickly. Clip and shape regularly. Because of its tendency to grow woody it should be replaced every four years. Sage does not like wet soil in winter.
Culinary use Particularly good with pork and veal dishes and with liver. Noted for its use in stuffings and sausage mixtures. Use sparingly.

Left *Because sage is particularly suited to rich meat, it has been a traditional ingredient of stuffings and marinades for centuries. A slightly unusual, but equally satisfactory, way of using the leaves is to wrap them around cream cheese to give additional flavour.*

This page, top *Savory, like most other herbs, is both useful and attractive.*

This page, centre *Although French tarragon is more difficult to grow than the Russian variety, it has greater culinary merit.*

This page, bottom *All thyme plants tend to straggle and need keeping in order.*

Opposite page, left *The leaves of both common and lemon thyme go well with veal or lamb. Sprinkle over meat before cooking.*

Opposite page, right *Use sprigs of fresh tarragon to add flavour to wine vinegar.*

Sorrel *rumex acetosa*
Perennial

Sorrel is like a cross between a herb and a leaf vegetable. Its leaves have a fresh, tangy, lemony taste.

Soil type Most light and well-drained soils.
Aspect Sunny.
Height 60cm(2ft).
Planting Sow seeds in spring in shallow drills.
Distance between plants 30cm(1ft).
Propagation Divide roots in spring or autumn and transplant.
Remarks Cut off the flowers to prevent the plant running to seed and becoming tough.
Culinary use Young leaves may be eaten raw in salad, later treat like spinach and use for soup or as a puréed vegetable.

Summer Savory *satureia hortensis*
Annual

Savory is a very useful, aromatic herb and looks like a long-leafed thyme. Summer savory has a subtler flavour than the winter variety which is perennial.

Soil type Moist soils if they are well-drained.
Aspect Sunny.
Height 38cm(15in).
Planting Sow seeds in spring or, as the seeds germinate slowly, buy small plants.
Distance between plants 30cm(12in).
Pot growth Will grow in a pot, needing an ultimate diameter of 15cm(6in).
Remarks As they do not give a very high yield it is advisable to grow several plants.
Culinary use Traditionally used with all bean dishes to increase flavour and make them more digestible. It is good in stuffings and casseroles and both leaves and flowers can be chopped into salads and soups.

Tarragon *artemisia dracunculus*
Perennial

There are two varieties of tarragon, French, which has the better taste but is difficult to grow, and Russian, which is hardier but has a tendency to spread.

Soil type Well-drained.
Aspect Full sun.
Height French tarragon 60cm(2ft).
    Russian tarragon 1m(3ft 6in).
Planting French tarragon can almost never be grown from seed but from root divisions or cuttings planted in spring.
Distance between plants 60cm(2ft).
Pot growth Can be grown indoors in pots with an ultimate diameter of 30cm(12in).
Propagation Either by root division in spring or autumn, or, in the case of Russian tarragon, allow it to seed itself.
Remarks French tarragon needs protection from frost. Do not cut died down growth until spring.
Culinary use In sauces, (Béarnaise is based on tarragon), to flavour

vinegar and with fish and egg dishes. It is particularly good with chicken dishes and in tomato and mushroom soups.

Thyme *common thyme: thymus vulgaris*
lemon thyme: thymus citriodorus
Perennial

There are several varieties of which the common and lemon are the most useful. Common thyme grows in the shape of a low bush and has strongly scented tiny leaves. Lemon thyme, along with several of the other varieties of thyme, is a short, creeping growth which spreads quickly and looks very attractive grown among paving stones, in pathways and terraces.

Soil type Most soils if they are well-drained.
Aspect Full sun.
Height 23cm(9in).
Planting Lemon thyme does not set seed, it is better to sow plant cuttings in early summer.
Distance between plants 23cm(9in).
Pot growth Can be grown indoors in pots needing an ultimate pot diameter of 20cm(8in).
Propagation Either buy new plants every two to three years or peg down peripheral branches and when they have grown independent roots, sever and transplant.
Remarks All varieties straggle and need replacing every few years.
Culinary use Used in stuffings, good with tomato dishes and with pasta.

The fruits of freezing

To be able to eat fruit which you know is really fresh and in peak condition is one of the many advantages of growing your own produce. To be able to eat the same, perfect summer fruit in the depths of winter is a delight only to be enjoyed by the gardener who also has a freezer. Not only will you save considerable expense by not having to buy what is fast becoming a luxury, but you will also be able to enjoy the experience of eating fruits which are rapidly disappearing from the open market. The increasing cost of labour and production involved in the hand picking of crops such as currants and gooseberries is leading to their gradual disappearance from greengrocers' shops and market stalls.

It is fortunate that most fruits, with the possible exceptions of the banana and avocado pear, do freeze well – indeed a thawed frozen raspberry is almost indistinguishable from a fresh one for colour, flavour and texture. As with the freezing of all other foods, it is important to follow a few basic rules:

Always harvest in perfect condition, when fully mature and well coloured.

Do not pick when wet, if this is possible.

Handle fruit as little as possible.

Always freeze as soon as possible after harvesting.

Do not wash unless strictly necessary, for example if you have sprayed the fruit with insecticide.

If you must wash fruit, do so in chilled water to help it remain firm.

The method of packing fruit depends completely on how the fruit is to be used. Rather than repeat the same information under each entry the basic methods are explained here.

Dry Pack This is suitable for fruits whose skins do not wrinkle, particularly soft fruits. It refers to the freezing of fruit which is packed without sugar or sugar syrup. The freezer life is somewhat shorter than for other forms of packing.

Dry Sugar Pack This refers to the packing of uncooked fruit which may first have been open frozen, but is anyway sprinkled with dry sugar. The sugar aids preservation by drawing out some of the oxygen and also forms a delicious syrup as it combines with the natural juices on thawing. The quantity of sugar obviously varies with the variety of fruit in question and individual tastes. Good for soft fruits.

Syrup Pack This is particularly suitable for light-coloured fruits which tend to darken quickly on cutting, such as peaches and pears. The syrup is made by heating water and sugar together until the sugar has dissolved, and leaving it to cool. The relevant proportions are given in the freezing instructions for each fruit. Do not boil the syrup. To save time when freezing, the syrup may be made a few days in advance and kept in the refrigerator until required. If a fruit is very prone to discoloration it is advisable to add either lemon juice or ascorbic acid to the syrup. Lemon juice may be added direct and stirred in. Ascorbic acid (vitamin C) is available in 500mg tablets

Left *Perfect fruit, fresh from the garden, is usually only a seasonal delight. Prolong that delight by freezing any surplus crops and enjoy them throughout the year. Unlike other methods of preserving, freezing does not noticeably affect the flavour of fruit.*

Above *Most fruit trees provide more than enough fresh fruit to satisfy the average family's requirements. Those that are not eaten immediately often have to be given away or left to rot. By freezing them you have a constant supply of fruit for sauces and puddings available at a moment's notice.*

or crystals from most chemists. One tablet or $\frac{1}{4}$ teaspoon of crystals should be dissolved in one teaspoon of water and added to each 1litre(2pint) of cold sugar syrup. Do not mix in copper or iron pans. The syrup should then be either poured over the fruit, which has been placed in a rigid container, until it just covers it, or poured in first and the fruit added as it is peeled and sliced. A piece of crumpled greaseproof paper or foil placed over the top will prevent fruit from floating above the syrup and turning brown.

Fruit may also be stewed, puréed or squeezed for its juice and then packed and frozen.

Fruit should always be thawed gradually in its container before being used. Soft fruits which are to be eaten uncooked should be served while still slightly frosty. Puréed fruit takes almost twice as long to thaw as whole fruit. Fruit to be cooked should be heated very slowly and fruit intended for pies must be thawed completely before use. A jam, incidentally, that has been made fresh from frozen fruit tastes considerably better than one which has been stored away for several months.

By growing your own fruit and freezing it you now have the opportunity to eat it fresh or to make puddings, pies, fools, preserves or delicious fruit salads, from a variety of fruit normally available for a short season only, which has been preserved in the best possible condition.

Fruit trees

A large proportion of the fruit included in this section is grown on trees. Before buying a tree it is important to decide not only which particular variety of fruit you wish to grow, but also the rootstock, because it is on this that the ultimate size of the tree depends. The various forms in which fruit trees are most commonly available are as follows:

Standard The natural free-standing form of a tree which has a central stem, or trunk of about 2m(2yds) from which the branches develop. Standard fruit trees can grow to enormous dimensions, particularly the cherry, and are therefore not recommended for the average garden.

Bush The main stem of a bush tree, which is free-standing, grows to approximately half the length of a standard and then divides into two or three main branches. As they are still capable of attaining a considerable size, it is more practical to buy a dwarf bush.

Pyramid A type of dwarf bush in which the branches start about 30cm(1ft) off the ground and as they radiate from the trunk become increasingly shorter so that it develops a conical shape. Although this type of tree bears fruit quickly it does require careful pruning.

Cordon A tree limited to a single stem, having no branches but only lateral shoots, which are pruned continuously to produce fruiting spurs. Cordons take up remarkably little space, but they must be supported. This can be done by training them at an angle of 45° either up a wall or on to wires stretched between stout posts. Many fruit trees, and also gooseberries and redcurrants, can be grown in this way, but it is not really recommended for stone fruits such as plums because of their dislike of heavy pruning.

Fan A tree which is trained to grow in a fan shape against a wall or post and wire supports.

Cordons, dwarf pyramids, espaliers and fan-trained trees are the most suitable forms for a garden. They all give a high yield in a limited space and are much easier to spray, prune and crop because of their shorter height. They do, however, require more specialized pruning to retain their shape.

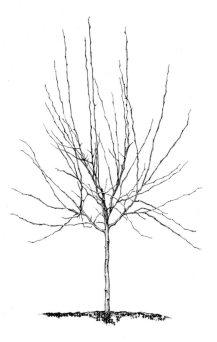

Pollinating

The other important factor to take into account before ordering a tree is the fertility of a particular variety. Some varieties are self-fertile, that is they set fruit with the pollen from their own blossom, and can therefore be grown singly. Others need to be in the vicinity of a complementary variety to provide cross-pollination in order to set fruit. Check that there is not a suitable tree in a nearby garden before ordering a second tree, but remember that they must both blossom at the same time.

The ideal soil type, aspect and method of cultivation are listed individually under each fruit. However, with the exception of the fig, the method of planting is always the same.

Planting

1   Prepare the planting site beforehand by removing all perennial weeds and breaking up the subsoil.
2   Trees should not be unwrapped unless you are going to plant them immediately. Instead, store them in their wrappings in a cool, frost-free place until required.
3   They should not be stored for more than a week. If you have to wait any longer before planting, heel them in. This means digging trenches deep enough for the roots to be covered in soil when rested at a slant in them.
4   Check that the roots are not dry. If they are, then soak them overnight prior to planting.
5   Remove any damaged roots and cut short those which are exceptionally long.
6   Hold the tree upright and estimate the spread of roots in order to determine the size of the planting hole. The depth of the hole should be such that the soil mark on the stem of the tree is level with the surface when planted.
7   Position the tree in the hole so that its roots are spread evenly around it. Fill the hole 8cm(3in) at a time, making each layer firm before adding the next one.

Free-standing trees must be supported and held in position with a strong stake until established. Drive this into place a few centimetres (inches) from the stem before filling the hole and secure the tree to it with adjustable ties. When planting cordons remember that they should be at an angle to the supporting frame and leave a space of about 20cm(8in) between root and wall where applicable. If the shoots are long enough, secure them to the wires or wall nails, otherwise tie them loosely to temporary stakes.

Finally, unless you are very strong, it is not wise to attempt planting single-handed. Get somebody to help you as it is a much simpler operation if one person holds the tree while the second person fills in the soil around the roots.

Top left *The majority of fruits, including the pears, peaches, plums and damsons in this picture, are grown on trees.*

Bottom left *A bush form of fruit tree. This is free-standing like the standard form of tree but the trunk is only about half the height.*

Below, left to right *A fan-trained, pyramid, cordon and espalier tree. These are the varieties of shape in which most fruit trees are available. Each type produces plenty of fruit but only takes up a small area. They do, however, require careful pruning.*

Apples

One of the most visually attractive of fruit trees when in blossom, the apple tree is also relatively easy to grow. Among the numerous varieties of this fruit, you are sure to find one which is exactly suited to your requirements.

How to grow

Soil Prefers deep loams, but will grow on sandy soils and heavy clay if you rectify their drainage deficiencies. It dislikes excessive nitrogen and benefits from being grown on a grass-covered site.

Aspect Sheltered and preferably frost-free, they need an annual rainfall of between 50–63cm(20–25in), although cooking apples will tolerate a heavier rainfall.

Planting In most gardens bushes, espaliers and cordons are the best forms to grow. Prepare the soil beforehand by digging over and removing all perennial weeds. Plant as for a fruit tree (see page 62) between autumn and spring, but preferably in autumn in order to get the trees well established before fruiting in 18 months time. Plant firmly, ramming the soil round the roots with the square end of a stout post and tie the tree to a substantial stake. Leave 30cm(12in) between bushes and 60–80cm(2–3ft) between cordons.

Cultivation Mulch the root area to conserve moisture during the first season, thereby minimizing the check to growth caused by transplanting.

Cordons should be pruned regularly by nipping out the growing points of all the side shoots when they have developed about three leaves. This usually happens by midsummer. New growths will rapidly replace them and these should also be pruned back in winter.

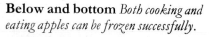

Below and bottom *Both cooking and eating apples can be frozen successfully.*

Bush forms of apple tree should be pruned in a similar sort of way – but treat each branch as a cordon.

Pests and diseases Although there are countless diseases which can attack the apple tree, most seem to thrive totally unscathed for 50 years or more. Protection from the larvae of the codling moth is effected by spraying with malathion, once when the blossoms fall and again three weeks later. The other more common complaint is apple scab, a fungus disease which appears initially as brown patches on the fruit. Remove and burn affected foliage and fruit in the autumn and spray with captan on the first appearance of the flower buds, again when the petals fall and finally when the immature fruits become visible.

Harvesting Apples are ready for harvesting when well-coloured, with the seeds becoming brown in colour, and when they part readily from the fruit spurs.

How to freeze

Preparation Apples can be successfully frozen in all of the following ways:

Uncooked – peel, core, cut into 1cm($\frac{1}{2}$in) slices and drop in water to which a pinch of salt or a squeeze of lemon juice has been added to avoid discoloration. Rinse before blanching.

Dry sugar – mix raw slices with sugar in the ratio of 125g(4oz) sugar to $\frac{1}{2}$kg(1lb) of fruit.

Syrup pack – prepare a syrup using 375g(12oz) of sugar to $\frac{1}{2}$litre (1 pint) of water and slice prepared apple straight into the syrup.

Purée – put slices of apple in a pan and add enough to water to prevent sticking. Cook until tender, rub through a sieve and cool.

Baked – cool.

Blanching Uncooked – 1 minute.

Packing Uncooked – open freeze and pack in plastic bags or rigid containers.

Dry sugar – pack in plastic bags or rigid containers.

Syrup pack – pack in rigid containers.

Purée – cool and pack in rigid containers.

Baked – cool, open freeze, and either wrap individually in foil or pack in large rigid containers and separate with interleaving.

Freezer life Uncooked, dry sugar, syrup packed and purée – 6 months.

Baked – 3 months.

To use All types of apple should be thawed at room temperature for 3 to 4 hours. Use as quickly as possible after thawing to prevent discoloration.

Top left *This fan-shaped apple tree has been trained to grow against a wall.*

Above *Just three of the numerous varieties of apple you can choose to grow in your garden.*

65

Above left *If you are planting a fan-trained apricot tree, it should be trained against a wall that faces the sun.*

Above right *Apricot halves that have been frozen in syrup can be used to make mouth-watering desserts.*

Apricot

The apricot tree is of Mediterranean origin and although hardy it flowers early leaving it vulnerable to frost. North of latitude 50°N or south of latitude 50°S, it should be grown in a greenhouse except in very protected areas.

How to grow
Soil Moisture retentive but well-drained and friable.
Aspect Frost-free and sunny.
Planting Apricots are self-fertile and may be planted singly. They bear fruit in their fourth year so buy a two- or three-year-old fan or bush tree. Plant as for fruit trees in soil to which 125g(4oz) of bone meal and 30g(1oz) of sulphate of potash has been forked. Plant in the autumn and leave 4.5m(15ft) between trees. Trees planted against a wall should be 23cm(9in) away and leaning slightly towards it. Tie central stem and branches of cordons to stout bamboo canes driven into the soil before planting.
Cultivation Give an annual spring mulch of manure around the base, plus a top dressing of 30g(1oz) of sulphate of potash per sq m(sq yd), taking care not to damage the roots near the surface. Water regularly the first season and subsequently in dry spells. Protect outdoor blossom from frost at night by draping soft fabric over it. Remove this by day to give access to pollinating insects. Assist pollination under glass by hand. Remove the blossom the first season.

Fruit forms both on young wood and old spurs. Prune and maintain a proportion of each in autumn, shorten the leaders by half to two-thirds after planting, laterals to a few centimetres (inches). Subsequently, shorten the leaders annually by one-third. Tie in one healthy shoot per 25cm(10in) of main branch in fan-trained trees, removing weak and upright-growing shoots, and pinch back the rest to four leaves from midsummer onwards.
Pests and diseases The same as for plums.
Harvesting Defer picking until the apricots are well coloured, ripe but not squashy and part readily from the spurs without tearing.
How to freeze

Left *Apricots that are to be frozen should first be washed and cut in half and then have their stones removed.*

Preparation Wash, do not peel, halve and remove stones. They can be frozen like this or in a dry sugar pack, allowing 125g(4oz) sugar to each ½kg(1lb) fruit, or in syrup made with a ratio of 375g(12oz) sugar to ½ litre(1pt) water, or if very ripe, cooked until soft in a syrup made with a ratio of 250g(4oz) sugar to ½l(1pt) water, or cooked until very soft in a little water, drained, sieved or strained, puréed and sweetened to taste.

Blanching Uncooked – ½ minute.

Packing Pack in rigid containers.

Freezer life All forms of apricot freeze well for 12 months except for purée, which is only really good for 3 months.

To use Thaw in their containers in a refrigerator for 3 hours at room temperature. Uncooked apricot may be eaten as it is, use others as required for puddings, desserts and jams.

Above *The raspberry has a reputation for being the ideal fruit to freeze, as, defrosted, the fruit retains both its colour and flavour to such an extent that it is difficult to distinguish from the fresh fruit.*

Cane fruits–*Raspberry, Loganberry and Blackberry*

The raspberry, loganberry and the cultivated blackberry are three soft fruits which for flavour and texture well reward any effort involved in their cultivation.

There are a few general rules which apply to the cultivation of all three fruits.

1　The soil should be well forked over prior to planting.

2　All perennial weeds, particularly bindweed and couchgrass, should be removed.

3　Organic fertilizer, such as farmyard manure, should be lightly forked into the surface to help water retention. Use up to 5kg(10lb) per sq m(sq yd).

4　Cane fruits may be planted either in the open or against a fence or wall. In the latter case, the canes can be secured by lengths of string tied to staples at the end of the row and at intervals of 50cm(18in) or so. A free-standing row, however, will require substantial posts at each end of the row and these should be put in before planting. Concrete or angle-iron posts make a good permanent job and should ideally be imbedded in concrete. Two lengths of strong wire should be fixed at 60cm(2ft) and 1.3m(4ft) from the ground.

5 Should the soil be too wet when the canes arrive from the nursery, heel them in temporarily in as dry a spot as may be available. If they arrive when frost prohibits planting, keep them wrapped up, and store in a cool shed where the roots will not dry out. Plant or heel them out as soon as conditions permit. If the roots appear at all dry when planting, soak them in a bucket for an hour or so.

6 A second layer of organic fertilizer spread over the ground after planting is advisable. This should be repeated annually at a rate of about 2.5kg(5lb) per sq m(sq yd).

Raspberry

Most raspberries bear red fruit but a few have white or yellow berries. Again most raspberries ripen in summer, but some varieties do not ripen until the autumn.

How to grow
Soil Lime-free, slightly acidic, well-drained and manured.
Aspect Full sun, but will tolerate some shade.
Planting Plant first-year canes 60cm(2ft) apart between the autumn and spring, but autumn is preferable. Too-deep planting is a common error with raspberries. The roots should be covered by no more than 8cm(3in) of soil. Immediately after planting cut back the canes to a height of 60cm(2ft) and finally lightly rake the soil to break up the surface.
Cultivation In spring, as soon as the growth buds begin to swell, cut back the canes still further – to a visibly live bud about 25cm(10in) above soil level. This is to leave just sufficient top growth to keep the roots active. No cropping must be permitted the first season and, after this cutting back, new suckers will spring up from the roots and these shoots are the ones which will fruit in the second season. Once these new shoots are growing well, the old 25cm(10in) high pieces should be cut down to soil level.

In the second summer, when the fruit has been picked, cut down all the fruited canes to soil level. These should have been replaced by new canes now springing up. If there are more than five or six suckers, select the best of even size and remove the rest. All prunings should be burned at once to prevent the spread of disease and pests.

The new canes should be tied in to the horizontal wires as they grow. In the following spring the canes should be tipped, making the cuts to growth buds some 15cm(6in) above the upper wire. This will stimulate better growth lower down where the berries are less liable to suffer wind damage.

Autumn-fruiting varieties should have the fruited canes cut out early in the following spring and the new growths will then fruit the same year.

Propagation This can be done by tip-layering in early summer, which involves pegging the tips of young canes down about 6–8cm(2–3in) deep, into small pots filled with a rooting compost and sunk in the ground. The young plants are severed from the parent canes when their roots have become established, in about early spring. Alternatively, root leaf-bud cuttings 5cm(2in) apart in a bed of sandy soil in a closed and shaded garden frame during the middle of the summer.

Top *The new suckers which spring up from the roots are the ones which will bear fruit the following season.*

Centre *After the old fruited canes have been cut down, the new canes should be tied on to horizontal wires as they grow.*

Bottom *Raspberries should not be allowed to fruit until the second season after planting.*

Each cutting should consist of a leaf and a bud with a 3cm(1in) length of cane bark devoid of pith. Roots are produced in three to four weeks; harden off the plants about a month later and transplant the following spring.

Pests and diseases In many gardens birds are probably the most destructive of pests and netting is the only sure means of defence.

Of insect pests the raspberry beetle is the worst. Other pests include the raspberry cane midge, the raspberry moth and aphids. The first two can be prevented by spraying with a five percent tar-oil wash in winter, and spraying or dusting with derris powder will protect the raspberries against aphids.

Raspberries are very subject to virus diseases but the health of commercial stocks has been greatly improved in recent years. For this reason it is particularly important to start by planting only canes obtained from a completely reliable source. There is no cure for these virus diseases. Affected plants should be dug up and burnt.

Harvesting Raspberries should be gently pulled from their central plug, unlike most other berries which are broken off. If pressure is required to do this, stop. The raspberry is not ripe.

Loganberries

Use loganberries for stewing, jam-making, bottling and wine-making. The ripe berries may also be eaten as a dessert, but may be too tart for some palates.

How to grow

Soil Rich, heavy and well-drained. Plants respond to a heavy annual mulch of organic fertilizer in the autumn.

Aspect Sunny but sheltered. Align rows from north to south.

Planting Plant either root tips or cuttings in early spring about 3m(10ft) apart and against fences, walls and up supports. On open sites use post and wire supports with wires at 60cm(2ft) distances from the soil level.

Cultivation Prune young plants back to 23cm(9in) immediately after planting to encourage the production of strong new shoots on which fruit will be borne the following year. Fruited canes should be cut down to ground level after harvesting and 10 to 12 shoots retained to produce the following year's crop.

Propagation As described under raspberries, this can be done by tip-layering in early summer, by leaf cuttings in the middle of the summer, or by rooted suckers in the autumn.

Pests and diseases These are the same as those which attack raspberries and should be treated in the same way.

Harvesting Loganberries are self-compatible and yield heavy crops of blunt, firm, very juicy, deep red berries. The berries do not plug so pick them when they are ripe, complete with core. One plant may produce between 7-8kg(15–17lb) of fruit.

Blackberry

The blackberry is a vigorous and exceptionally spiny hardy perennial variety of cane fruit, whose crop is used for desserts, tarts, jams and wine. A single plant provides sufficient fruit for most households.

How to grow

Soil Rich, well-drained soils.

Aspect Sunny and sheltered.

Planting Buy first-year plants and plant in the autumn. If you wish to grow more than one plant, leave 3m(10ft) between them. Prune them back immediately to about 23cm(9in). If they are replacement shoots train them to one side of the fruiting canes to avoid contamination with fungus diseases. If you are planting them for the first time, train them up a wall, wire fence, or in the open tied to suitable supports.

Cultivation With only one or two exceptions, e.g. 'John Innes Berry', blackberries form fruits in their second year. After fruiting, cut off as much of the old wood as possible in order to allow the new shoots, either growing off old wood or from the ground, room to manoeuvre. Leave up to 10 new shoots and destroy any that are surplus. They will require both watering and feeding during the summer.

Propagation The same as for the other cane fruits, that is by tip-layering in early summer, by leaf cuttings in mid-summer or by rooted suckers in the autumn.

Pests and diseases If they develop crowngall or stunt virus, destroy them. Treat greenfly with derris powder.

Harvesting The fruit should only be harvested when the berries have turned a purplish-black and can be detached from their cradles with ease. One plant may produce up to 7kg(15lb) of fruit.

How to freeze

Preparation Perfect, ripe, dry fruit, may be frozen as it is. Fruit which is slightly damaged in some way, should be made into a purée.

Remove and discard any remaining hulls, do not wash unless absolutely necessary. Fruit – open freeze whole fruit. Purée – place the fruit in a sieve set over a bowl and, using the back of a wooden spoon, rub the fruit through. Add sugar to taste in the proportion of about 125g(4oz) sugar to ½kg(1lb) of fruit. Stir until the sugar has dissolved.

Packaging Tip the open-frozen fruit into a plastic bag when it is hard, and seal. Pour the purée into rigid containers leaving a headspace and seal.

Freezer life 12 months.

To use Thaw fruit for six hours in a fridge or at room temperature for three hours. Purée can be thawed either by leaving for about three hours at room temperature, or, when time is short, by standing the container in a pan of warm water.

Far left, top *The loganberry is a vigorous plant, producing long whippy runners and big juicy berries with a distinctive flavour.*

Far left, bottom *Loganberries can be propagated by tip-layering. Here the bud has already started.*

Below left *Freezing your fruit will allow you to enjoy treats like blackberry and apple pie throughout the year.*

Below right *The blackberry is particularly spiny, but wearing gloves to protect your hands when picking fruit is a good idea with any cane fruit.*

Cherries

There are two main kinds of fruiting cherry, the sweet and the sour or Morello cherry. All varieties, except for the Morello, suffer from two disadvantages. Most sweet cherries are self-sterile and therefore you need to grow another compatible variety nearby for the purposes of cross-pollination. Secondly, there is no dwarfing rootstock available and a mature standard cherry is probably too large for the average garden, reaching a height of about 15.2m(50ft) with a span of 12m(40ft).

How to grow

Soil Light to medium loam with good drainage and no risk of waterlogging, and preferably frost-free.

Aspect Sweet – full sun, Morello – away from the sun.

Planting As standard trees are so large, the average gardener will find it more convenient to plant bushes or fans. Young trees, not exceeding five years old, transplant best. As cherry trees do not fruit until their sixth year, buy and plant four-year-old trees, if you can get them, which are easier to train and reduce the waiting period. Plant during the dormant season, as for fruit trees, 4.5m(15ft) apart and stake securely. Fans which are to be trained against walls should be planted with the stem 23cm(9in) away from the wall and leaning slightly towards the wall, securing any branches which are long enough to wall nails or wire, with soft ties.

Cultivation Shortly after planting, shorten the previous season's growth on the leading branches by half, and side shoots to 8cm(3in).

Cherry trees grown in the open benefit from an annual spring mulch of manure and give fans grown against walls a spring feed of general fertilizer at a rate of 60g(2oz) per tree. Regular watering is necessary to prevent the fruit from splitting.

Sweet cherries fruit chiefly on the spurs formed on the older wood. Pruning consists of preserving the open shape of the tree together with removing dead and weak growth and thinning overcrowded branches. Pruning should be minimal and confined to the spring and early summer to avoid attracting fungal diseases.

Sour cherries fruit on shoots formed the previous season. After the basic fan of branches has been established by shortening the leaders each year as for sweet cherries, annually replaced side growths are tied in parallel to the permanent branches. Cut overcrowded laterals leaving about 15cm(6in) between each, and those growing at right angles to the wall or trellis. When pruning fan-trained sweet cherries, allow the main branches to extend as far as possible but otherwise prune in the same way.

Pests and diseases Protect from birds with netting and control blackfly on appearance by spraying with pyrethrum.

Harvesting Fruit should be left on the tree until it is completely ripe. Sour cherries should be cropped by cutting the stalks with a pair of scissors as the bark tears easily.

How to freeze

Preparation All cherries should be washed, dried and stoned. Sweet cherries may either be frozen as they are, or in a dry sugar pack using 125g(4oz) sugar for each ½kg(1lb) of fruit, or covered in a syrup made in a ratio of 375g(12oz) sugar to ½l(1pt) water or gently simmered for 15 minutes in a syrup made in a ratio of 250g(8oz) sugar to ½l(1pt) water. Sour cherries should be simmered for the same amount of time but in a syrup made to a ratio of ½kg(1lb) sugar to ½l(1pt) water.

Packing Pack in rigid containers.

Freezer life 12 months.

To use Thaw at room temperature for 3 hours before use.

Left *The season for eating ripe, juicy cherries is all too brief. Freezing is the best way to preserve them for any length of time.*

Below *Cherries should always be left on the tree until they are completely ripe.*

Bottom *The formation of fruit on a cherry tree is always heralded by a profusion of exquisite, delicate blossom.*

Above left *Although red currants are excellent eaten raw with a little sugar and cream, their sweet-sour flavour is the ideal complement to dark meat and game in the form of red currant jelly.*

Above right *The black currant is really too sour to eat raw, but cooked with added sugar in desserts, jams and syrups it is both delicious and nutritious.*

Currants – *Black currants, Red currants and White currants*

There are three types of currants: black currants, derived from *Ribes nigrum*, red currants, derived from the cross-breeding of three *Ribes* species and white currants, derived from red currants. All three are self-fertilizing, fruit prolifically and take up only a relatively small area of the garden. All varieties of currant are worth growing and freezing as, because of the difficulties involved in picking them, they are very expensive to buy.

How to grow

Soil Well-drained but moisture-retaining. No soil is too rich for black currants; they can be fed lavishly with nitrogenous fertilizers and will absorb copious amounts of water. Red and white currants withstand drought better than black currants and are less greedy for nitrogen.

Aspect Sunny and sheltered. Red and white currants blossom early and must not be planted in low-lying frost pockets.

Planting The modern method of planting currants is to insert three cuttings 10cm(4in) deep and allow about 2m(6ft) between them. This space is needed both for picking and pruning, but many other plants, such as salad vegetables, may be grown between them. Take cuttings in autumn with as little delay between the removal and insertion of the cuttings as possible. Cuttings take readily, may be grown *in situ* and allowed to fruit in their first season.

Alternatively, plant one-to-two-year old bushes during the winter. Position them deep enough for all shoots to arise from the soil. Transplanted bushes should be pruned by shortening the shoots to four buds in order to help them recover quickly and to induce strong growth. Prior to planting the soil should be dug deeply and have 50kg(1cwt) of well-rotted manure dug in every 18sq m(10sq yd).

Cultivation Feed black currants in the spring with 60g(2oz) per sq m(sq yd) of sulphate of ammonia or nitro-chalk and in the autumn with 30g(1oz) per sq m(sq yd) of sulphate of potash. Red and white currants manage with 30g(1oz) of sulphate of ammonia per sq m(sq yd) in spring and the same amount of potash in the autumn.

Propagation All varieties have a productive life of up to 12 years, but if new bushes are needed this can be achieved by taking cuttings. These should be about 30cm(12in) long and taken in the autumn from well-ripened shoots of the same season's growth. It is unnecessary to make the cuts directly below the nodes as the cuttings root readily wherever the cuts are made.

Pruning Black currant bushes fruit on the previous season's shoots and should be pruned as soon as their crop is harvested. Remove most of the stems which have produced the fruit and leave the fresh new shoots to fruit the following year. Red and white currants fruit on the spurs of old wood and should be pruned in winter by shortening the leading shoots by a third and the side shoots to two or three buds. Summer pruning promotes fruit bud formation. Shorten the side shoots to five leaves and leave the leading shoots unpruned.

Black currants are grown as stools after planting but red and white currants can be trained to make a standard bush or grown as cordons.

Harvest Remove in small bunches and strip off the fruit with a wide-pronged fork. Black currants may be harvested by removing branches bearing fruit and stripping them at a table. A certain amount of wastage is inevitable when harvesting as currants nearest the base of a truss ripen before those at the tip.

How to freeze
Firm ripe fruit may be frozen for eating uncooked, for cooking or making preserves. Surplus and slightly imperfect fruit can be made into juice and frozen.

Preparation Fruit – Wash if necessary and pat dry. Do not bother to remove stalks as these break off after freezing. Open-freeze in small bunches. If you wish to freeze them with sugar, allow about 125g(4oz) of sugar to ½kg(1lb) of fruit. If you intend to use them later for jam, it is advisable to blanch them first for 2 minutes otherwise their skins may toughen.

Juice – Place the fruit in a saucepan allowing ½l(½pt) water to each ½kg(1lb) of fruit. Bring the water to the boil and remove the pan from the heat after one minute or the flavour and vitamin content will be impaired. Pour the contents of the pan into a scalded muslin bag suspended over a bowl and allow the juice to drain through overnight. Measure the juice and add 375g(12oz) sugar to each ½kg(1lb) of fruit. Stir well until the sugar has dissolved.

Packaging Fruit – Tip the fruit into plastic bags and seal. Juice – Either pour into rigid containers leaving a headspace and seal. Alternatively, pour the juice into an ice tray, remove the cubes when they are frozen and either wrap each cube in foil or keep them all in a plastic bag and seal.

Freezer life 12 months.

To use Either thaw overnight in the fridge or for about three hours at room temperature for raw fruit. Fruit that is intended for cooking does not need to be defrosted.

Top *The white currant is less commonly grown than the other varieties although, like the red currant, it has an attractive flavour and may be eaten raw.*

Above *As black currants do not fruit on old spurs, but on new shoots which have sprung up the previous season, the task of cutting out the fruited canes and harvesting may be carried out at the same time.*

Above left *The fig tree is unusual in that the fruit forms in the late summer and survives through the winter to mature the following year.*

Above right *The fruit of the fig may be frozen whole to be eaten raw later, or in a syrup so that it is ready for cooking.*

Figs

Figs grow most successfully in areas with a typically Mediterranean climate, but, with care, they can also be grown in areas of temperate climate which have mild winters. Mild winters are important because the fruit of the fig tree forms in the summer, and survives through the winter to mature the following year.

How to grow
Soil Poor and shallow.
Aspect Very sunny and sheltered from the cold in winter. In cool, temperate climates, grow against a wall facing the sun or in a cold greenhouse.
Planting In cooler climates, order pot grown trees from the nursery. Plant in spring bearing in mind that fig trees have an ultimate spread of 3.5m(4yds) and height of 2.5m(8ft). Take this into account if planting more than one tree. Dig a deep hole 1m(3ft) square and line the bottom and sides with bricks to restrict root growth. Fill the hole up with ordinary garden soil to which ½kg(1lb) of bonemeal has been added. Remove the tree from the pot and plant it firmly in the middle. In countries with warmer climates, this is unnecessary.
Cultivation Keep newly-planted trees regularly supplied with water until they are well established. No pruning is needed, except pinching out vigorous young shoots or removing in spring any frost-damaged or dead wood. In cool temperate climates protect the tree from severe weather by covering with sacking or other coarse material, and packing straw around the base, keeping the whole lot dry by fixing a sheet of plastic firmly to the wall. Before packing, remove all the larger fruits from the tree and discard, as they will not be ready at the right time and will only use up valuable strength. This does not apply to trees grown inside.
Pests and diseases There are no pests to worry about, but figs can succumb to a variety of diseases of which botrytis and dieback are the two most common. These only occur in cool temperate climes as they are precipitated by frost damage. Other than keeping the plant well protected there is little you can do to prevent it. If either occur, cut off the branches to 15cm(6in) beyond the affected area, remove any rotting fruit and destroy both.
How to freeze
Preparation Wash perfect, unsplit fruit in chilled water and cut off

the stems with a sharp knife. Either leave whole, peeled or unpeeled, or prepare a syrup in the proportion of 250g(8oz) sugar to $\frac{1}{2}$l(1pt) water to cover halved fruit.

Packing Open freeze unsweetened whole fruit and pack in rigid containers. Pack halved fruit in rigid containers and cover with syrup.

Freezer life 12 months.

To use Thaw at room temperature for 2 hours. Unsweetened fruit may be eaten raw, or used for making jam. Sweetened fruit should be cooked gently in its own syrup.

Gooseberry

The gooseberry is native to Britain, where it has been cultivated since the thirteenth century. It prefers temperate climates. Being self-fertile and productive, it is ideal for the small garden. Another reason for growing it is because it is not often available on the open market.

How to grow

Soil Most soils which are well-drained, not prone to water-logging and not deficient in potash.

Aspect Sunny and frost-free ideally, but will succeed even in partial shade but not in tropical areas.

Planting Gooseberries may be grown as bushes, cordons or standards. The latter two are easier to crop but all give a good yield. Plant the rooted cuttings from which they are propagated from late autumn to the end of winter. Bushes and standards should be set out 1.2–2m (4–6ft) apart, cordons 60cm(2ft) apart. Cordons should be trained up a fence or wall. Plant firmly, spreading out the roots and then covering them with 8–10cm(3–4in) of soil. Shorten the leading shoots by a half and side shoots to two buds.

Cultivation Give a generous mulch in the spring and thorough waterings in dry spells during the first summer. Keep the soil weed free by hoeing shallowly to avoid damaging the surface roots. Feed every spring with 30–60g(1–2oz) per sq m(sq yd) of sulphate of potash.

Pruning Bush varieties should be pruned to six leaves per side shoot in summer before blossoming and any suckers torn out. Prune again in winter by shortening leading shoots by one third and side shoots to 4cm(1$\frac{1}{2}$in). Keep the centres of the bushes open to facilitate cropping. Cordons should be pruned as for red currants.

Pests and diseases Protect from birds with netting. Remove the larvae of the gooseberry sawfly by spraying with derris.

Harvesting Harvest the berries when they are under-ripe for cooking or when fully coloured and soft for dessert use.

How to freeze

Preparation Freeze either whole and uncooked, as they are or in syrup, or as a purée. Uncooked – top and tail and wash if necessary. Syrup – top, tail and cover in a syrup made in the proportion of 375g(12oz) sugar to $\frac{1}{2}$l(1pt) water. Purée – simmer in as little water as is necessary until tender. Rub the fruit through a sieve or strainer and sweeten to taste.

Packing Pack plain fruit in plastic bags and fruit in syrup and puréed fruit in rigid containers.

Freezer life 12 months.

To use Thaw plain fruit for one hour at room temperature before cooking or making preserves. Fruit in syrup may be cooked gently direct from the freezer, in the syrup. Purées should be thawed either overnight in the refrigerator or at room temperature for 3 hours before use.

Top *Gooseberries which are to be cooked should be picked before they soften.*

Above *Gooseberries make superb pies but are equally good for making jam and wine.*

Top *Grapes should be assessed for picking on the maturity of the bunch as a whole.*

Above *Grapes fruit prolifically, but for a really good crop a sufficient number of immature bunches must be removed to allow those remaining to develop.*

Grapes

Grapes are available in the shops throughout the year but are worth freezing for convenience. They can also be grown successfully outside, even in temperate climates.

How to grow

Soil Most fertile, well-drained soils to which a little bonemeal has been added.

Aspect Sunny, sheltered and preferably frost-free. Against a wall facing the sun is a good spot.

Planting Plant at any time throughout the winter, choosing two-year old pot grown plants from a nursery, if you can get them. Break the pot to avoid damaging the roots, open the soil ball carefully and spread the roots out in the hole which should be wide enough to take the roots spread to their full extent. Plant firmly about 1.2m(4ft) apart, and, immediately after planting, prune the young plant to within 30cm(12in) of its base.

Cultivation Plants out of doors are best grown as cordons, espaliers or fans. The cordon consists of training the shoots which arise from the plant on a trellis or on a horizontal wire framework about 1.2m(4ft) high. Fan shapes should be grown against a wall and 5–8 shoots from the main stem trained to grow on a wire framework. In both cases, the shoots should be loosely tied to the wires or trellises, spreading them well apart. Vines also grow well trained over pergolas.

Water the young plant regularly during dry periods in its first season until it is well established. Each winter, give a generous mulch of manure and a dressing of general fertilizer. Mature plants only need watering and feeding on rare occasions.

Vines grow prolifically and should be pruned rigorously but carefully, especially when the fruit is ripening in order to allow the sun to reach it. Allow only one bunch of grapes to grow for each 30cm (12in) of lateral stem and remove the rest. Lateral shoots must be pruned back in winter.

Pests and diseases Spray plants in midwinter with tar/oil emulsion to remove any insects. Specially ventilated bags can occasionally be obtained in which to enclose ripening fruit in order to protect it from wasps.

Harvesting Grapes should be assessed for picking on the maturity of the bunch as a whole.

How to freeze

Preparation Except for seedless grapes which may be frozen whole, skin, cut in half and remove the pips. Prepare a syrup of 250g(8oz) of sugar to $\frac{1}{2}$l(1pt) water.

Packing Pack in rigid containers and cover with the syrup.

Freezer life 12 months.

To use Thaw at room temperature for 3 hours. Grapes to be added to savoury dishes should be drained well first. Grapes for fruit salad may be added with or without the syrup.

Peaches and Nectarines

The peach is closely related to the apricot, cherry and plum. The nectarine is a mutated peach with smaller, more delicately flavoured fruits.

How to grow

Soil Well-drained, medium loams. In heavy clay, add lots of compost and break up the subsoil to aid drainage.

Aspect Abundant sunshine and preferably frost-free. In temperate climes they thrive under glass and may also be grown successfully outside against sun-facing walls.

Planting Prepare the planting area by adding 1.25kg(2.5lb) per sq m (sq yd) of coarse bonemeal to the soil. Plant trees in late autumn or winter and cover with no more than 10–15cm(4–6in) of soil, tread firm and ensure that the graft union is above ground. Keep fans 10cm(4in) away from walls and leaning slightly towards them, and tie temporarily until the soil has settled. Planting distances are: for fan trees 4.5m(15ft) apart and for bush trees 4.5–6m(15–20ft). Mulch either with compost or strawy manure in spring and rub off the first season's blossoms.

Cultivation Water newly-planted trees during dry weather and repeat mulching each spring. Protect wall trees from frost where necessary by covering at night with fabric but removing it by day to allow pollinating insects access to the flowers.

Pruning When pruning, remember that these trees fruit on the previous year's shoots. As the fruit swells new shoots appear at the base of the fruit-growing shoots. Rub off all but one on each shoot during the summer. Cut out the fruited shoots after harvest and tie in the replacements in fan formation 8cm(3in) apart.

Pests and diseases Protect from birds with netting. Peaches and nectarines are prone to many diseases of which one of the most serious and most common is peach leaf curl. This causes the leaves to shrivel, develop red blisters, turn white and finally fall. Prevent by spraying the tree and the immediate locality with Bordeaux mixture late winter and autumn.

Harvesting Leave the crop to ripen fully on the tree and test for maturity by smelling and pressing lightly at the stalk end.

How to freeze

Preparation Prepare a sugar syrup in the ratio of 250g(8oz) to ½l(1pt) water and add ascorbic acid to it. Peel, halve and stone the fruit under cold running water and add immediately to the syrup.

Packing Pack in rigid containers.

Freezer life 12 months.

To use Thaw in the container in a refrigerator for 4 hours. Serve while still frosty.

Top *If you do not have time to make jam when peaches are in season, freeze them and make it when you are less busy.*

Centre *Fan-trained trees often set an excessive crop, and the fruitlets should be thinned progressively to allow the remaining fruit room to ripen.*

Bottom *The nectarine has a smooth skin quite unlike the rough downy skin of the peach.*

79

Pears

Pears have been cultivated for centuries, indeed Pliny, the Roman writer, knew of 39 distinct varieties. There are now literally hundreds of varieties, most of which emanate from Europe. However, as a variety which stores well has still not been developed, the only way to preserve them for any length of time is by freezing.

How to grow
Soil Pear trees do not like extremes of soil type and grow best in medium, rich loam.
Aspect Sunny, protected and preferably frost-free.
Planting Pear trees may be grown in every form open to fruit trees, but because of their size it is better to buy and plant either cordons or dwarf pyramids. Find out whether the species you want to grow is self-fertile or needs another variety for cross-pollination before ordering. Plant as for a normal fruit tree between late autumn and spring, preferably as soon as possible after the leaves have fallen. Prepare the soil beforehand by dressing with manure or compost and a couple of handfuls of bonemeal. Plant cordons 2m(2yds) apart, allow to slope towards the wall or wires and tie loosely to the wall fastenings or wires. Plant pyramids 2.3m(7ft) apart and loosely tie them to a stake.
Cultivation The subsequent manuring of pear trees should be adjusted according to performance but all trees benefit from an annual spring mulch of rotted manure, left on the surface to a depth of about 5cm(2in), and pricked in with a fork the following autumn.

Prune cordons by pinching out new side shoots in midsummer and trimming particularly long ones in autumn to 10cm(4in). The pyramid should have its lateral branches pruned back in summer.
Pests and diseases As for apple. Also attacked by fireblight which first causes the flowers to blacken and the twigs to die and then begins to affect the branches. Cure by cutting off wood beyond the affected area and burning it.
Harvesting Pick dessert pears as soon as they begin to soften. Overripe pears quickly deteriorate.
How to freeze
Preparation Pears are best frozen slightly cooked. Peel, quarter and remove the core. Add the pieces to a syrup made in the proportion of 250g(8oz) sugar to $\frac{1}{2}$l(1pt) water, which may be prepared beforehand. Poach for $1\frac{1}{2}$ minutes, drain and cool.
Packing Pack in rigid containers with enough of the cooking syrup poured over to ensure that the fruit is covered.
Freezer life 12 months.
To use Thaw in its container in a refrigerator for 3–4 hours and use as required.

Top *Serve dessert pears with the cheese board for a perfect end to a good meal.*

Above *As harvesting approaches, branches which are heavily laden with greengages will need the support of padded wooden props.*

Plums, Greengages and Damsons

Plums are popular for cooking, jam-making and bottling, but the sweeter varieties are among the most delicious of dessert fruits. Damsons ripen a little later than most plums and their fruit is not normally sweet enough to be enjoyed raw, although it is excellent cooked or preserved. Greengages are simply a class of plum with a characteristic, and particularly delicious, flavour. Greengages and damsons are grown in exactly the same way as plums.

How to grow
Soil Well-drained and containing plenty of humus. Dig in compost or manure but do not add any lime.

Aspect Preferably frost-free and facing the sun. They like a rainfall of between 50 and 90cm(20 and 35in) although damsons will succeed in areas with higher rainfall, and less sunshine, than plums will tolerate.

Planting As no satisfactory dwarfing rootstock is yet available and a standard or even bush tree is too large for most gardens, it is best to buy and plant fans, for wall-training or against the support of posts and horizontal wires. Plums do not produce fruit until the fourth or fifth year so buy a three-year-old fan if possible. Plant as for fruit trees in spring or autumn.

Cultivation Do not allow the ground to become dry until the tree is well established. Give a light mulch of compost or manure every spring, and prick this lightly into the surface the subsequent autumn. When established, dress the tree each spring with 30g(1oz) of nitro-chalk per tree and 15g($\frac{1}{2}$oz) of sulphate of potash. Every third year, add 30g(1oz) per sq m(sq yd) of superphosphate. Only prune if branches are weak or overcrowded. Do this in summer and coat the cut surface with a fungicidal paint.

Pests and diseases Spraying during the winter with a tar/oil wash will cure aphis, which is seen to be present either by the leaves curling up or from sooty deposits on and around the tree. Silver leaf, a fungal disease, causes the leaves to turn silver and then affects the branches. Cure by cutting branches 15cm(6in) beyond the affected area, paint and destroy the wood.

Harvesting Dessert plums should be left on the tree until quite ripe and then picked from the stalk. Cooking plums should be picked when they begin to colour.

How to freeze

Preparation Plums, greengages and damsons should all be wiped, halved and stoned. They may then be frozen as they are, packed in sugar to taste, in a syrup made from 375g(12oz) sugar to each $\frac{1}{2}$l(1pt) of water, or stewed in the normal way.

Packing Pack in rigid containers, remembering to pour over the sugar or syrup where necessary.

Freezer life 12 months.

To use Thaw overnight in a refrigerator in the covered container to avoid discoloration. Untreated fruit may be used for cooking and preserves, or eaten on its own after simmering in a syrup. Plums in sugar may be eaten raw. Plums in syrup may be drained and used for cooking, or simmered from frozen in its own juice until tender. Stewed fruit should be gently reheated.

Below *The dark purple fruit of the damson is normally too tart to be eaten without being cooked with sugar.*

Bottom *Spread home-made plum jam over sweet pancakes for a quick and economical dessert.*

Quince

The somewhat acidic flavour of the quince is an acquired taste which is worth developing. It is almost pear-shaped in appearance, with a yellowish skin and a pungent aroma. The tree itself is known for its longevity and the beauty of its pale pink flowers.

How to grow
Soil Any really moist soil.
Aspect Sunny and sheltered.
Planting Plant the bush variety, as the standard can grow to quite a size, and stake as for a fruit tree. If you wish to grow more than one, leave 3.5m(20ft) between them. Plant in the autumn.
Cultivation Mulch generously in the spring after planting and water regularly during periods of dry weather until the tree is well established. Remove any branches which appear to be weak in order to promote growth.
Pests and diseases None to worry about.
Harvesting Leave to ripen on the tree for as long as possible. If there is a danger of frost, remove the fruit and leave it to finish ripening inside.

How to freeze
Preparation Quince may be frozen either uncooked or cooked. Uncooked – wash, peel, cut into quarters and remove the core. Cooked – simmer slices until tender in a little water to which has been added the peel and the juice of two oranges. Dissolve sugar in the proportion of 375g(12oz) to ½kg(1lb) fruit. Strain and reserve the syrup.
Blanching Uncooked – 2 minutes.
Packing Open freeze uncooked quince and pack in plastic bags. Place cooked quince in a rigid container and pour over the strained syrup.
Freezer life 12 months.
To use Thaw at room temperature for 3 hours. Stew uncooked quince and add to apple pies and pear dishes or use it to make preserves. Cooked quince can be added to desserts made from apples and pears as soon as it has thawed, or serve it on its own.

Top *The flesh of the quince, when raw, is yellow like its skin, but turns pink after cooking.*

Above *Do not begin to harvest rhubarb until the sticks have turned pink.*

Right *Young, tender pink sticks of rhubarb make the best pies, purées, fools and jams.*

Rhubarb

Although rhubarb is strictly a vegetable, because its edible stems are treated as a fruit, it has been included in this section.

How to grow
Soil Well-cultivated, rich soils.
Aspect Open and sunny.
Planting Prepare the site by removing all perennial weeds and digging it over deeply. Add manure at the same time at the rate of 50kg(1cwt) to 9sq m(10sq yds). Buy crowns or sets which have at least one good fat bud, and plant in the spring, autumn or winter. Plant firmly in holes which are deep enough to leave the pink buds immediately below the surface. Leave 1m(1yd) between each plant.
Sowing Some varieties of rhubarb can be raised from seed, but as you have to wait two years before being able to use it, this method is less satisfactory. Sow outside in cold frames in spring in 3cm(1in) deep drills. Thin seedlings to 15cm(6in) apart as soon as they are large enough to handle. Transplant to the specially prepared bed the following spring.
Cultivation Do not pull sticks in the first season after planting, but encourage the plants to become firmly established by watering during

periods of dry weather and giving occasional feeds of liquid fertilizer. Hand weeding should be carried out in the first season, but after that the large leaves inhibit the growth of weeds and make it unnecessary. To ensure that the plants continue to crop well, mulch the bed each autumn and remove flower stems on appearance. Rhubarb plants only need replacing every ten years.

Pests and diseases None to worry about.

Harvesting Rhubarb may be picked throughout the growing season, but it is at its best when young, tender and pink. Do not pull too many sticks at one time as this weakens the plant. Pull by holding the stick near the base and then twist and jerk upwards at the same time. Do not harvest by cutting or breaking the stems.

How to freeze

Preparation Rhubarb may be frozen uncooked, in syrup, stewed or as a purée. Uncooked – wash trim and slice. Syrup – prepare a syrup of 250g(8oz) sugar to $\frac{1}{2}$l(1pt) water. Stew – as you would for eating fresh. Purée – stew sliced rhubarb in the water left on it from washing it and rub through a sieve or strainer, or blend in an electric liquidizer.

Blanching Uncooked – 1 minute.

Packing Pack uncooked in plastic bags, and all other forms in rigid containers.

Freezer life 12 months.

To use Uncooked rhubarb may be cooked straight from the freezer in a pan, with just enough water to prevent it from sticking and sugar in the proportion of 125g(4oz) to each $\frac{1}{2}$kg(1lb) of fruit. Heat rhubarb in syrup gently straight from the freezer until it is tender. Stewed, puréed and uncooked fruit which is to be added to pies or eaten as a dessert, must be thawed for 3 hours at room temperature before use.

Below *Only perfect, even-coloured strawberries should be selected for freezing.*

Top right *Use cages or netting to protect strawberries from birds.*

Centre right *Help protect fruit from mud and slugs by tucking straw under each group of berries.*

Bottom right *Summer fruiting strawberries may be brought on earlier by protecting them with glass or polythene cloches.*

Strawberry

Strawberries are of two main types; summer fruiters and perpetual fruiters or alpines. Both are reasonably easy to grow and equally delicious to eat.

How to grow
Soil Rich, medium loam with a high humus content. Well cultivated and drained.

Aspect Sunny but ideally protected from frosts and winds. Alpines will tolerate a little shade.

Planting Prepare the soil beforehand by digging in manure at 5kg(10lb) per sq m(sq yd). Plant summer fruiters in early autumn in soil prepared the previous summer, and perpetual fruiting and alpine varieties in spring or autumn. For spring planting, the soil should be prepared the previous winter. Alpine varieties may also be grown from seed sown in spring in a greenhouse and planted out in early summer.

Use a trowel for planting and dig a hole deep enough to accommodate the roots without bending them. Then return a little soil to the centre of the hole to make a mound on which the strawberry plant can 'sit' with its roots spread evenly around it. Plant firmly, using the handle of the trowel as a rammer, and make sure that the base of the crown is at soil level. Plants may either be kept spaced out with runners removed or left to matt and the runners pegged down. Plants to be spaced out should be planted in rows 1m(1yd) apart at 45cm(18in) intervals. Leave 15cm(6in) less room both ways if you want them to matt. Summer fruiters may be brought on earlier by protecting them with cloches.

Cultivation It is advisable to pick off blossoms on very young plants to promote growth for a better crop the following year. Dress strawberry plants with fertilizer each spring and then mulch with manure, compost or peat. Water regularly during long periods of dry weather.

Not long after the berries begin to develop, runners will appear. Unless these are required for propagation, they should be cut off at once with a pair of scissors so as not to waste the plant's energies.

Pests and diseases Protect from birds with netting and from slugs by scattering slug pellets. Botrytis, which may occasionally develop, particularly in very humid conditions, causes brown patches to appear on the leaves initially and finally reduces the entire plant to a grey, mouldy heap. This can be prevented by spraying the flowers when they first open, and again a week later, with a fungicide, and by keeping down weeds and ventilating cloches. Plants which are already infected should be promptly removed and destroyed.

Harvesting The fruit should be picked by taking the stem about 1cm($\frac{1}{2}$in) behind the berry between finger and thumb. In this way the berry can be broken off without being touched. Pick regularly and only select perfect even-coloured fruit for freezing.

How to freeze
Preparation To help avoid mushiness in thawing, choose only small, firm, dry berries and hull but do not wash them. Either leave them as they are and open freeze them or cover them in syrup made in the proportion of 375g(12oz) sugar to $\frac{1}{2}$l(1pt) water. Alternatively, rub them through a sieve or strainer to form a purée and sweeten to taste.

Packing All strawberries should be packed in rigid containers.

Freezer life 12 months.

To use Thaw in their containers at room temperature for 3 hours. Serve whole strawberries while still slightly frosty or use for puddings and preserves. Use puréed strawberries for making fools, sauces and ice-creams.

A glossary of gardening terms

Blanching
The protection of a vegetable from exposure to light. Usually accomplished by drawing up the earth around the plant to cover the part to be protected e.g. see potato and celery, or by covering with cloth, black plastic sheeting or boxes e.g. chicory.

Compost
Term for all kinds of soil mixtures used for raising seedlings or growing pot plants when qualified and elsewhere to refer to organic fertilizer.

Cutting
A piece of a plant taken from stem, leaf, bud or root and planted so that it will put out roots and grow into a new plant. It is one method of vegetative propagation.

Derris
A vegetable-based insecticide effective against raspberry beetles, caterpillars, wasps and red spider mites. It is poisonous to fish so must be kept away from pools. Of short persistence.

Dibber
Small tools with a thin, blunt end, used for making planting holes. Ideal for making holes for small plants but not bulbs or potatoes.

Drill
Shallow furrow made in the soil in which seeds are sown.

Harden off
Gradually accustoming plants raised in protected conditions to outside temperatures and ventilation. If the process is too hurried, growth is checked and leaves can show signs of bad health.

Lateral
A side growth, either a branch or a shoot. When pruning, make sure you distinguish between laterals and leading or terminal shoots, often known as the leader which is at the end of the branch. Laterals are usually cut back harder than leaders.

Layering
Pegging a long healthy shoot to the ground after making a short cut through joint (or node), so that plant will root from this area into earth.

Malathion
An organophosphorus insecticide useful in the control of aphids, scale insects, thrips, beetles and fruit tree red spider mites. Sweet peas, fern and zinnias are plants that can be damaged by use of the spray. Of short persistence.

Mulch
Insulating layer of various materials put over soil to prevent loss of water by evaporation. Some mulches also feed the soil slowly.

Nicotine
A vegetable-based poison useful as an insecticide against aphids, capsids, sawflies and leafminers. Extremely poisonous to humans when in the concentrated state. Mark POISON; store under lock and key and never decant into harmless-looking containers. Of short persistence.

Node
Point in stem from which a leaf grows.

Organic
Derived from decaying natural (i.e. once-living) substances.

Prick out
To lever seedlings out of their seed box as soon as they can be handled and to transplant into deeper seed boxes with slightly richer soil.

Pyrethrum	Useful and safe insecticide, particularly when combined with derris to produce a product of short persistence.
Rootstock	The root system on which a cultivated variety of plant has been budded or grafted.
Tuber	Enlarged part of a root or underground stem lasting a year only.
Variety	Plant varying from typical form of a species, in colour, shape or habit. Used commonly about any plant differing from the typical form.

A glossary of freezing terms

Ascorbic acid	Vitamin C, a synthetic form of which is available from most chemists. It is added to syrup used to pack fruit to prevent discoloration. Directions for its use are given in the introduction to the fruit section.
Blanching	The immersion of vegetables in boiling water before freezing to retard the action of enzymes. A detailed explanation of the process is given in the introduction to the vegetable section.
Cross-flavouring	The introduction of the flavour of one food to another. This is caused by inadequate packaging.
Enzymes	Chemical substances which are present naturally in all food. In vegetables which are not blanched they cause deterioration in flavour, colour and texture.
Fast freezing	A method of preserving both flavour and texture more efficiently which is more fully explained on page 8.
Headspace	The space left at the top of a container when freezing liquid and semi-liquid foods e.g. soups and purées. Liquids expand when frozen and failure to leave such a space, which should be about 1cm($\frac{1}{2}$in), will result in the container being forced open and the quality of the contents being allowed to deteriorate.
Interleaving	The placing of pieces of greaseproof paper or foil between layers of food to allow for easy separation.
Moisture-proof and vapour-proof wrapping	Wrapping which is non-porous and therefore protects the food from dehydration.
Open-freezing	Also called free-flow freezing. Fruits and vegetables are spread over a tray, uncovered, and placed in the freezer until hard. They are then packed in plastic bags or rigid containers and deep frozen. Food frozen in this way will remain completely separate. This has the advantage that if you do not wish to use the complete amount you can tip out only the quantity that you require and return the remainder to the freezer.
Thawing	The process by which food that has been deep frozen gradually returns to room temperature. Not all fruits and vegetables, especially those which are to be cooked, require thawing.

Index